# Hidden Worlds:
## young children learning literacy
## in multicultural contexts

# Hidden Worlds:
## young children learning literacy in multicultural contexts

*Clare Kelly*

**Trentham Books**

Stoke-on Trent, UK and Sterling, USA

Trentham Books Limited

Westview House     22883 Quicksilver Drive
734 London Road    Sterling
Oakhill                VA 20166-2012
Stoke on Trent      USA
Staffordshire
England ST4 5NP

First published 2010

British Library Cataloguing-in-Publication Data
A catalogue record for this book is available from the British Library

ISBN 978 1 85856 459 3

Designed and typeset by Trentham Books Ltd and printed in Great Britain by Henry Ling Ltd, Dorchester.

# Contents

## Acknowledgements

This book would not have been possible without the help and support of many people.

Firstly I would like to thank the six children and their families who were so generous in sharing their private worlds with me, and the staff of the Nursery for allowing me to observe their knowledge and skill at first hand.

I would like to thank Eve Gregory for her support over many years, for sharing her wisdom and always asking the questions that helped me move on.

I am very grateful to my colleagues at Goldsmiths, a wonderfully talented and dedicated team of people. I particularly want to thank my friends on the English team for our frequent invigorating and thought-provoking discussions. I feel very privileged to have been able to engage with their knowledge, expertise and vision, which has influenced me in so many ways.

I would like to thank Charmian Kenner, Kathy MacLean, Nikki Mellor and Heather Mendick for their generosity in reading and responding to the manuscript and for their insights, comments and suggestions; Panna Begum for her knowledge and skills as an interpreter and Shane Herbert for the cover photograph.

Thank you also to Gillian Klein for her editorial skills and belief in the book and to Chris as always, for all his support and encouragement.

Dedicated to Chris, Beth, Ruth and Gemma

# 1
## Researching literacy in context

*Sabina, dressed in a beautiful midnight blue sari greets me warmly and takes*
*me to the living room of their flat. The three children are lying on the floor*
*drawing while half watching a children's cartoon about animals while their*
*grandmother looks on, talking to them encouragingly in Sylheti-Bengali. Kabir,*
*clearly embarrassed by seeing me in this setting, for the moment at least, is*
*pretending to be a dog and won't say hello.*

This book is about young children's understanding of literacy. It tells the
stories of three boys and three girls and their families and takes a view
of literacy as a complex human activity rather than a set of skills to be
learned. The children's literacy experiences took place in their homes and
local communities in the company of close family members and were part of
the day to day activities and relationships that constituted family life.

When the children went to nursery, they were venturing into the world away
from their families for the first time. In a new environment geared for large
numbers of children, they encountered new literacy experiences and also
new forms of relationships with adults and other children. They knew a great
deal about literacy in the familiar world of home and this became more obvious as they began to make links with their experiences in the new context
of the nursery. Observations of their play and self initiated activity demonstrated that they were actively involved in making these connections and
developing their own learning in collaboration with other children and
adults. Because of this configuration between home and school, each child
had a unique orientation to literacy.

The division between literacy at home and school has sometimes been seen
as the reason why some children are not successful in formal education. Chil-

dren from families where certain key experiences such as being read a bed-time story do not take place, are often seen as losing out. Bourdieu's concept of cultural capital (1997) is used to explain why some children fit easily into school and others do not. Liz Brooker (2002) examines his theory in relation to young children starting school. Bourdieu argued that the match between cultural experiences at home and at school gave children differential access to school practices and the values, attitudes and ways of talking that were integral to them. This familiarity would affect each child's adjustment to school and ultimately their educational success. Since school practices were normally synonymous with those of the middle class, children's social class was often a significant feature for their success at school. This book concentrates on the connections children make between their experiences, rather than identifying directly what they need to know when they come to school.

The past fifteen years or so have seen the growth of family literacy programmes that are based on the premise that young children will experience greater success at school if certain school related activities such as storybook reading are introduced to their families. Jackie Marsh (2003) has shown that this is often a one way process: home practices are discounted. Carol Edelsky (1996) argues that the potential of family literacy programmes for finding out about home practices has never been realised and instead programmes have been imposed which devalue families' real experiences.

Most of the children discussed in this book did engage in what could be termed school literacy practices with their families; most were involved in sharing and talking about books, many were learning the English alphabet, most were experimenting with making meaning on screen or on paper. These practices took place in most homes but the relationship between them and the children's understanding of their place in the nursery was not straight-forward. The stories here suggest that it is not necessarily the home literacy experiences that count for success in the nursery but rather what children make of them, with support from adults and peers.

The snapshots I present of the children at home and in the nursery reflect the complexities of literacy learning and the multiple models of literacy that can evolve, co-exist and combine in families. Some of the children were learning to be literate in two or three languages and scripts, and could use language interchangeably according to text and purpose. They had understood that texts should be treated with different degrees of respect and reverence and that some could have significance for how to live your life. Many of the children were learning that literacy is a source of family pride and associated with the security of life and relationships at home and in countries far away.

Examining the children's experiences at micro level revealed how their understandings of literacy were rooted in their family history and particularly their parents' experiences. As the adults' lives changed according to their circumstances, new definitions led to new forms of literacy and literacy learning which became part of the children's experiences. Literacy was thus far more than a skill but linked to children's identities as family members, which changed and evolved over time.

## The study

This book emerged from a wider study into literacy learning (Kelly, 2008) which was conducted in a large urban nursery in a densely populated area of London. It predated recent recommendations for the teaching of reading in the Foundation Stage which are discussed in Chapter 9, but addresses their implications.

I visited the nursery for a morning each week over one year and made field notes and audio recordings and took photographs. Informal interviews were conducted with children, family members, teachers, nursery nurses, nursery assistants and the head of the nursery unit. Family members were asked to keep a participant diary of literacy related activities.

Many studies (Taylor and Dorsey-Gaines, 1988; Minns, 1997; Volk and de Acosta, 2004) have captured the everyday stream of incidents and activities in the family that impact on children's understanding of literacy. While acknowledging this background, my main aim was to observe and talk to parents about their children's literacy activities at home, because I believed they reflected their beliefs and values about literacy and would reveal the distinctive ways it was modelled, experienced and learned in the home.

I aimed to see literacy learning from the perspective of the children and to try to understand how they made sense of their experiences at home and in the nursery. As a former early years teacher, what I discovered led me to question some long held beliefs about early years practice.

Being a researcher put me in a privileged position, giving me access to the worlds of home and the nursery. However, I could only ever capture a small part of the children's literacy experiences. And I am aware that in telling the stories of the children and their families, I am claiming to represent groups of people with whom I do not share a language or culture. This position has inherent problems and limitations.

## The nursery

In the nursery where the study took place, children were treated as emergent readers and writers who already knew a great deal about literacy when they arrived. The key role of the adults was to plan the environment based on their understanding of how children learn, their knowledge of child development and their observations of children's interests and progress. Staff interacted with children to mediate their learning and make it more explicit through their use of language.

Aims were clearly laid out in a booklet for parents and families and divided into aims for the children and principles for teaching and learning. Aims for children included the development of confidence, independence and self esteem and a sense of respect and responsibility. There were certain guiding principles including the centrality of learning through play, belief in parents as partners, respect for social and cultural experience, belief in the value of talk, first hand experience and a positive approach to learning. There was also an explicit commitment to show positive respect for differences in culture, race, religion and language of all ethnic groups represented in the school.

The language policy, also made available to families, was divided into sections that covered speaking and listening, reading and writing, and in each case specified aims, principles of planning and examples of various activities that were likely to take place with groups and individuals in the nursery. There was a strong emphasis throughout on the place of story as a unifying mechanism and a vehicle for developing all language modes. Nursery staff identified the consistency of approach and shared principles as a reason for wanting to work in the school.

The walls were covered with children's drawings, models and mark making as well as digital photographs of individuals or groups engaged in various activities. Artefacts made by the children were suspended from the beams that ran across the ceiling. Children moved comfortably and safely and were encouraged to take responsibility for choosing activities both inside and outside and where necessary selecting appropriate resources. There were two computers in the room and a wide range of software. Children operated the computers independently and their popularity was evident from the length of the list nearby which children signed if they wanted to use a machine.

## Staff views on literacy

The staff worked hard to support the children's learning in all areas. They gave generously of their time and energy to enhance the children's experiences, to ensure a safe, settled and stimulating environment and to recognise and meet children's individual needs. Their understanding of child development and their interest in the children was evident in their day to day interactions with them, and in the written and informal observation they made. They were busy, conscientious practitioners, each with their own tacit as well as explicit understandings of literacy.

In common with most early years practitioners at the time, the nursery staff were subject to pressures from outside the classroom to change their practices and influenced by competing views about how children become literate and what constituted success. A public dialogue was intensely focused on the inadequacy of current approaches to teaching reading and especially early literacy, with the news media stressing the importance of teaching what they called 'the basics'.

Pressure came from outside the nursery to teach literacy in a more structured and formal way. One member of staff called this a 'fight' and a 'battle'. Education professionals disagreed about the most productive ways for young children to learn to read and write. Proponents of a child centred perspective emphasised the importance of children learning from authentic activities that stressed meaning and purpose, while those who favoured a more structured approach believed that attention should be paid to the skills involved

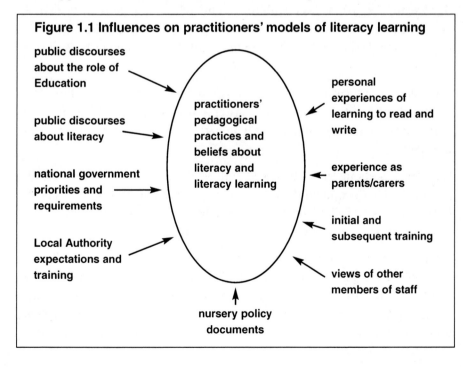

**Figure 1.1 Influences on practitioners' models of literacy learning**

public discourses about the role of Education

public discourses about literacy

national government priorities and requirements

Local Authority expectations and training

practitioners' pedagogical practices and beliefs about literacy and literacy learning

personal experiences of learning to read and write

experience as parents/carers

initial and subsequent training

views of other members of staff

nursery policy documents

and urged the teaching of phonics. During the study external pressures and centrally driven initiatives impacted on the Early Years curriculum, creating pressure for more formal teaching of isolated skills. This culminated in the Rose Report (DfES, 2006) which advocated the *Simple View of Reading* with its emphasis on the teaching of synthetic phonics for all young children.

Interviews and informal discussions with staff showed that their views on literacy learning were a combination of their professional training, their own experiences of becoming literate and their experiences as parents. Day to day observations and encounters with children in the nursery and the discussions at planning and assessment meetings had also influenced their philosophy. But it was also clear that they were influenced by the external pressures and constraints calling on them to change their practices.

## A guide to the book

Chapter 2 discusses sociocultural theory and literacy learning, exemplified in an analysis of a story reading event where the nursery teacher helps the children to take meaning from a picture book. The concept of 'the third space' is introduced to explain the metaphorical place where the children were able to make connections between home and school.

Chapter 3 focuses on Kabir, who was aged three years and eight months when the research began. He lived with his mother who is Bangladeshi-British, his father who came to England from Bangladesh and his two older sisters. The family's main language is Sylheti-Bengali and the children spoke English to each other.

Chapter 4 introduces Michelle, who was four years and one month old. She lived with her mother and teenage sister and was part of a large extended family of aunties and grandparents who had come to the UK from Jamaica in the 1960s.

Chapter 5 is about Sadia, who was four years and three months old. Her parents had both come to the UK from Bangladesh five years before she was born. She spoke Sylheti-Bengali and English to her two older sisters and Sylheti-Bengali to her parents and younger brother.

Chapter 6 introduces Jamie who, at four years and four months old, is the eldest of the six children. He lived with his mother and grandmother who had resided in the area around the nursery all their lives. When he was younger, Jamie had been cared for by his grandfather who had been a great storyteller and Jamie was steeped in an oral tradition passed down over generations.

In chapter 7 we meet Nicole at age four years and one month. She lived with her mother, two older brothers and sister. Her mother was born in the UK to parents who had come from Montserrat. Nicole had close and frequent contact with her extended family, including grandmother, aunties and cousins.

Chapter 8 focuses on Asif, who was aged three years and three months. He lived with his parents who had come from Dhaka in Bangladesh when Asif was one year old and they were temporarily living in the UK while his father studied for a Law degree. He spoke mostly Bengali at home and some English.

Chapter 9 examines the main issues that arose from the children's experiences of literacy at home and in the nursery and the commonalities and individualities that their stories revealed. Suggestions are offered for policy and practice that might help practitioners to reflect on the opportunities they create to help children make connections between their different worlds.

Although this book is primarily about literacy, it is also about young children's learning, more generally. The emphasis is on respecting the experiences children bring to school, which is so important for developing relationships in which children feel valued, included and positive about themselves.

### Notes

All names used in the book are pseudonyms.

Although the term parents is used, it is intended to represent carers and others who have responsibility for children.

# 2
# Literacy as a social and cultural activity in homes and schools

*The book of the week is* The Enormous Turnip. *It is read aloud each day by the adult who is on the rota to do large group storytime. Today copies of the book are put out with story props for children to use to tell their own story. There is a tape recorder and set of headphones and an accompanying tape which has been recorded in English on one side and Bengali on the other. A small group of children are acting out the story with masks while Margaret (nursery nurse) is reading the book. This is being videoed for all the children to watch later on the computer. Some children are mark making for a wall story of the book. There is a display of sunflower seeds planted by the children with an open information book* From Seed to Sunflower *next to it, Some children are cutting up vegetables including turnips, in preparation for making soup which everyone will drink later.*

This snapshot of the nursery where my study took place was typical of the staff's approach to literacy learning. Story was a springboard for other activities and literacy was a social activity with a purpose rather than just an end in itself. However, many of the experiences the nursery children were enjoying were particular to a school context. It is unlikely, for example, that they would have multiple copies of a picture book at home or be writing a wall story with others or have books opened out on a table as part of a display. In this chapter I look at a sociocultural approach to learning because it highlights the significance of context for children becoming literate.

## A sociocultural perspective on learning
Socioculturalists highlight the individual nature of learning experiences. The following chapters show how literacy learning is dependent on each child's

environment and takes place within the shared beliefs and practices of their community. This perspective contrasts with, for example, those of people who see learning as moving through predetermined stages of development, who are likely to be more concerned with identifying the knowledge and skills involved at each point.

Sociocultural theory is rooted in the work of Lev Vygotsky (1978) and his view that learning and thinking have their basis in social relationships where experiences are shared. He argued that children come to understand and think about the world alongside people who are important to them and that this process is mediated by language. Children learn firstly on a social level through using language in personal interactions with others, but later that language becomes internalised on a psychological level and this allows them to use it to develop new meanings and ways of behaving. Explained in this way, psychological development has its basis in social relationships and practices and ways of understanding the world. So Vygotsky argued that children's intellectual development cannot be explained separately from the experiences of those beside whom they learn and whose own understandings are located in the social, cultural and historical influences on their community

From this perspective, young children are seen as apprentices to more experienced adults or peers who guide them into traditions, routines and ways of understanding the world that are shared in their family and beyond. For example, the degree of respect given to older members of a community varies between cultures. This is something young children learn by watching and listening to others and by participating in interactions themselves. It is unlikely that anybody will explicitly spell out such attitudes and values to children, but they will learn them alongside others, using forms of language that signal respect or deference, impatience, tolerance etc. Through participation with others, young children learn these shared values and understandings about the older generation which guide their actions and ultimately their thinking on how to categorise them, as they encounter new situations and relationships.

Louis Moll and his colleagues (1992) have characterised the experiences, skills and understandings that we all hold from encounters with significant people as contributing to our 'funds of knowledge' which determine the ways we see the world. They argue that some children's funds of knowledge will find a match with school practices, but for others those funds will not count and they will have to learn to keep them separate.

Vygotsky believed that for learning to occur, the child's participation in social interactions must take place at a comfortable yet challenging point. He termed the gap between what the child can do on their own and what is possible in collaboration with a more mature adult or peer: the 'zone of proximal development' (ZPD). The ZPD enables the child and the more skilled person to accomplish a task together which is then internalised by the child, later practised alone and then generalised to new situations.

'Scaffolding' has been used as a metaphor to show how learning takes place in a socially mediated activity within the ZPD. Wood, Bruner and Ross (1976) were the first to explain how interaction routines can support the development of knowledge and skills. They argue that scaffolding involves retaining the complexity of a task while simplifying the learner's role. Mediators guide or model an activity, based on what they know the learner can do, and change the focus of that intervention as the learner's skill increases, until they can do alone what could formerly only be done with support. For example a child may be unable to complete a jigsaw on their own, but an adult or child may guide them by suggesting they look for the corner pieces, or edges, or pieces that are the same colour. Initially, this will give the child strategies to complete the jigsaw together with their mentor. Through repetition and practise over time, the child comes to understand the significance of these and other strategies and takes more responsibility for them so they can eventually complete the jigsaw independently and then transfer what has been learned to completing a different jigsaw.

More recently the notion of scaffolding has been developed to take account of the subtleties involved. Barbara Rogoff's concept of 'guided participation' (1990, 2003) emphasises the cultural variations in the dynamics of the process and the ways in which the active participation of the less experienced partner can directly affect the process on both a social and psychological level. Rather than just internalising the view of the experienced partner, Rogoff argues that there is a co-construction of meaning and that through this active involvement, children take on an understanding of their own of an activity or process. An example of co-construction is discussed later in this chapter.

## A sociocultural approach to literacy learning

Vygotsky suggested that because reading and writing are social practices, literacy has to be understood by looking at how it is used in life. He argued that children's understandings of what literacy was for came from both observing and participating in day to day activities that involve reading and writing. Researchers have documented all the different, often ephemeral ways that children observe literacy going on around them in family life (Leichter, 1984; Weinberger, 1996; Cairney and Ruge, 1998). Eve Gregory and Ann Williams (2000) have written about how children are directly involved in literacy activities in conjunction with adults and other children.

In these situations, socioculturalists argue that children come to understand the activities and how they are used. For example Kabir, one of the children in the book, saw his father regularly write letters to family members in Bangladesh. It is likely he would notice that they were written on special paper and set out in the same way each time, written in a script that was used in the family but not on television, and that he too could take part by writing his name at the end. When the replies came bringing family news, they were read out and talked about. By observing or participating in an important literacy activity in the family, Kabir was learning how to use language for a specific purpose and also sharing the roles and relationships that were central to it. Later in this chapter we see an example of a literacy event in the nursery and a different set of roles, expectations and behaviour.

This emphasis on the form and function of literacy activities and values that surround them is perhaps best understood by looking at the work of Shirley Brice Heath (1983). She carried out a renowned ethnographic study of three rural communities in the Piedmont Carolinas and found each to have distinctive ways of using and taking meaning from texts and socialising their children into an understanding of literacy.

The people of Trackton engaged in a range of literacy practices with children that included storytelling, rhymes, songs and verbal-play which reflected the rich oral culture of the community. Reading materials were mainly connected to church related activities the community felt were important, so the storybooks the children encountered when they started school were unfamiliar because they had no place within the community culture. The focus on the written word for the people of Trackton was in relation to the message it carried. When they started school, children were being asked to enter fictional worlds through stories and ways of talking about them that were not only outside their previous experience, but were also not valued by their community.

Roadville residents read to their children but did not consider it necessary to make explicit connections between the book and their children's lives. They believed that books which gave children information were more important than fiction. Adults and children spent time together working on alphabet and number books and reading bible stories. At these times, children were often asked factual questions to check their understanding. They were told stories grounded in reality and these were often a reminder of how to behave. When they began school, the children encountered familiar interactions with number and alphabet books but found it increasingly difficult to meet the expectation that they should make links between texts and their own experience.

The Townspeople saw books as an important medium for learning and set aside time for reading and talking about stories and relating them to everyday life. They used books with children for labelling and as a focus for asking and answering questions and they modelled the uses of literacy in other settings outside the home. When children went to school they met many similar practices and settled easily into school literacy learning.

Heath's work was significant because it

- highlighted variations in practices and the uses of literacy between the three groups
- explained the norms and values attached to literacy learning and the social rules the children were introduced to
- demonstrated the links between oral and written language and how this relationship was distinctive within each community
- described the congruencies between community and school based literacy practices and the consequent impact on children's success at school.

### Understanding change

A sociocultural perspective is also useful for the purposes of this study because it recognises the importance of the history of a culture. The practices of the three communities in Heath's study evolved over time and were related to the circumstances in which they lived, worked and prayed. This sociohistoric view of literacy learning takes account of what has been important about literacy to a community in the past, what is significant for its members in the present but also how their beliefs about literacy might shape learning in the future. The children in this book, as we shall see, were engaged in a dynamic process of moving forwards into new ways of being literate, but always with an eye looking back over their shoulder to ways of engaging with literacy which were rooted in their family history.

## The New Literacy Studies

The New Literacy Studies (NLS) is a movement that flourished in the1980s, following major research that showed how communities lived and worked with different literacies depending on the purpose and place where it occurred (Scribnor and Cole, 1981; Street, 1984). Proponents of the NLS spoke of context as critical to understanding the nature of literacy because it imposed its own purposes, functions, values and behaviour. Street suggests:

> Every literacy is learned in a specific context in a particular way and the modes of learning, the social relationships of student to teacher are modes of socialisation and acculturation. The student is learning cultural modes of identity and personhood, not just how to decode script or write in a particular hand. (1995:140)

They spoke of literacies in the plural, as integral to different contexts. Consequently it was proposed that literacy is a set of practices used in different ways by individuals, groups and communities. Such a view immediately distances definitions of literacy as an autonomous, universal and neutral skill that needs to be first learned and then applied in any context, such as the home, workplace or school.

David Barton applies an ecological metaphor to literacy. He explains:

> Rather than isolating literacy activities from everything else in order to understand them, an ecological approach aims to understand how literacy is embedded in other human activity its embeddedness in social life and in thought and its position in history, in language and in learning. (2007:32)

The New Literacy Studies show that there are different domains of literacy, domestic, work, leisure, religion, and that school literacy is one form. It has a higher status because of its connection with the institutions of school and university, rather than because of any intrinsic superiority. Proponents of the NLS argue that because in school, reading and writing are taught in a logical, ordered and objectified way, school literacy is seen as more scientific. In home contexts it is learned through participating in events where literacy is integral to an activity rather than an end in itself.

The focus on literacy as a social and community practice rather than a school-based skill demands that it is conceived of more broadly than the ability to read and write. James Gee (1996, 2000) has written powerfully about the social and cultural significance of literacy. He makes the point that the practice cannot be divorced from the text since one will always read and write something and different texts will require particular skills and background knowledge.

The work of the New Literacy Studies links literacy to 'personhood' and identity (Street 1984, 1995). Other researchers have talked about children's 'literate identities' (see Kenner, 2000, 2004; Marsh, 2005; Drury, 2007) This is helpful for the purposes of this book. Firstly it represents how deep rooted these conceptions of literacy are, because they carry with them ways of acting, behaving and thinking that impact on the child's sense of who they are. Secondly because it explains how children who come to school with one set of experiences and practices from home can learn to make sense of and internalise a new set of expectations and beliefs. The children we meet in Chapters 3 to 8 were engaged in making connections between their experiences in different literate communities in new ways that would contribute to their literate identities.

### *Literacy events and literacy practices*

If we make a distinction between literacy events and literacy practices, literacy can be understood as a system rather than a skill. The term literacy events arose most prominently from Heath's study. She identified all the occasions where reading or writing were used by people in their lives. On many of these occasions, she notes, particularly in the context of home, talk will surround and be a central part of the activity.

The construct of literacy practices was developed by Brian Street to distinguish both the ways in which literacy was used and the social routines and ideological beliefs that surrounded a literacy event. In other words, each literacy event will have an associated literacy practice which refers to the particular expectations, values and attitudes that are integral to it. James Gee points out that the same text can be read in different ways and the meanings that can be taken from it will be dependent on the literacy practices that surround it.

> A way of reading a certain type of text is only acquired, when it is acquired in a 'fluent' or 'native-like' way, by one's being embedded (apprenticed) as a member of a social practice wherein people not only read texts of this type in this way, but also talk about texts in such ways, hold certain attitudes and values about them, and socially interact over them in certain ways. (1996:41)

These ideological aspects of literacy will connect the literacy event to other similar literacy events for members of the same community, and to wider societal forces such as school, work or religious institutions. In the following examples Nick, the nursery teacher in the study, is reading a story to a group of three and four year olds. We can see the ways that a set of literacy practices is integral to a literacy event and linked to what is seen as desirable in the wider society.

## Reinforcing expectations at story time

It is the end of a busy morning, before lunch and after 'tidy up time'. The older children left the nursery to join the Reception class in September and the new intake of much younger children is in the process of settling in. Most of them are sitting on the carpet with their legs crossed. Nick sits in a chair facing them, holding up a copy of *The Elephant and the Bad Baby*. Linda, the nursery nurse, encourages the other children to finish clearing up and sit down ready for the story.

**Figure 2.1 Learning expectations in a nursery literacy event**

| Nick | Children |
|---|---|
| 1.   Can you remember what you do at storytime? | |
|      Do you need to be | |
| 5.   touching someone else now? | |
| | Samia: No |
|      No because they don't like it. | |
| 10. | Harry: Touch your own body |
|      Touch your own body – yes! Look with your eyes. | |
| 15   Yesterday we read *The Elephant and the Bad Baby*. Do you remember how the story started? | |
| 20 | Michelle: He found a friend |
|      Yes he found a friend. What did he do Yasmin? | |
| | Yasmin: He went |
| 25 | Rumpeta, Rumpeta, Rumpeta. |

Nick and the rest of the staff have created this context for reading a storybook. It is consistently planned for every morning and afternoon, over the course of a week, given importance through clear labelling and accompanied by a specific set of behaviours and expectations – *Can you remember what you do at storytime?* (line 1). This deliberate routine with explicit expectations, demonstrates to the children that there are particular ways of interacting around texts: ways of sitting, concentrating, paying attention and talking about books, that are encouraged and rewarded. It is the Autumn term, these children are still very young, many are not yet four. They are at the early stages of learning how to interact with texts in a large group in the nursery. Some children respond to Nick's questions, others watch him and the book closely.

The pattern of the interaction is dialogic in nature; questions are asked and answered and children are encouraged to take turns. Lines 4-9 and 15-25 reveal the routine of question, response, feedback, although line 10 with Harry's suggestion of *Touch your own body* shows that children are also per-mitted to make their own contributions. Reading the story is a collaborative venture, a social experience and a negotiation between the adult and children who are encouraged to participate in *What did he do Yasmin?* (line 22) and are actively involved in the process. The staff are introducing and reinforcing specific expectations about ways of behaving that are common in the school context and although they may well reflect ways of reading storybooks in some homes, they will be unfamiliar in others because this is one way of read-ing but not universal practice.

### Reading beyond the words

The following literacy event took place later in the year with older children who had more experience of storyreading in the nursery. Nick is reading *The Three Little Wolves and The Big Bad Pig* and helping the children to draw on a range of information to make inferences from the text.

The children are sitting on the carpet. Nick is facing them holding the book. The story focus for the past two weeks has been *The Three Little Pigs*. Children have had the opportunity to hear, retell and act out the story and there have been a range of related activities. So they are familiar with the conventional story and are judged ready for this subversive version which reverses the role of the protagonists.

Nick is scaffolding the children's reading of the text by simplifying their task so they can participate in a complex process of understanding the meaning through a combination of words and pictures. As he reads the story he

## Figure 2.2 Learning how to make sense of a picture book

| Nick | | Children | Text |
|---|---|---|---|
| 1 | Now...What do you think happened next ...in the story? | The big bad... | |
| | | Leyton: the big bad... | |
| 5 | Someone over here? Joachim what do you think happens next... in the story? Aysha? | The big pig is gone. | |
| 10 | | Aysha: The big pig is gone | |
| | The big pig is gone? | | |
| | | Jake: He's come back. | |
| | Let's find out. (*turns back to book*) | Leyton: There he is | |
| 15 | | He came back. | |
| | | Jamal: He's playing football. | |
| | Oh yes, they're playing tennis. Over | | |
| 20 | here (*points to picture*) Yes. | Children: Look, look, look. | |
| | And look, here's the pig, looking over the | The fox is there (*lots of | |
| 25 | wall. Can you see? | voices – excited, indistinct*). | |
| | Here he is. Oh my goodness. Shall we read on and find out | | |

| Nick | Children | Text |
|---|---|---|
| what happened?<br>(*taps the book*) | | |
| | Kadeisha: He's sleeping | |
| 30 OK Right. Put your hands in your lap please. | | |
| (*reads*) No sooner than they had finished<br>35 that the BIG BAD PIG (*slow articulation, loud voice*) came along down the road. And he saw the house made of ....? | | No sooner had they finished than the big bad pig came prowling down the road and saw a house of concrete that the little wolves had built. |
| 40 | Concrete.<br>Concrete.<br>(*all*) concrete. | |
| Shahina, a house made of concrete. | | |
| 45 Yes, they were playing a game outside. | | They were playing battledore and shuttlecok in the garden and when they saw the big bad pig coming, they ran inside their house and shut the door. |
| | Leyton: Tennis<br>Kadeisha: It's a garden. | |
| 50 The pig rang the doorbell. Get ready everyone<br>(*puts up hand to ring imaginary bell*). | | The pig rang the bell and said, 'Little frightened wolves, let me come in!' |
| | (*children raise hands*)<br>Ding Dong! | |

| Nick | | Children | Text |
|------|------|------|------|
| | Ding Dong (*loud, high pitch*). | | |
| | | Ding Dong! Ding Dong! | |
| 55 | That looks like a garden doesn't it Kadeisha,you're right. And – I wonder what he said. Can you | | |
| 60 | guess? Can you guess what he said? | Mohammed: Come in. | |
| | Little frightened wolves can I come in? (*sing song voice*) | | |
| | Get ready. No, no, | | |
| 65 | no. I can't hear you (*puts hand to ear.*) | | |
| | | Leyton: No, chinny chin chin. | |
| | No, no, no. Not by The hairs on our | | No, no, no said the three little wolves. By the hair |
| 70 | chinny chin chin. We'll not let you come in. | | on our chinny-chin-chins, we will not let you in, not for all the tea leaves in our china teapot. |
| | | Chn: No, no, no (*clapping and shouting*) Chinny, chin, chin. | |
| 75 | | Leyton: That will frighten the bad pig. | |

monitors the match between the children's understanding and the words of the text. He tries to overcome any misunderstandings by re-working or omitting anything he considers to be potentially problematic. For example the children are unlikely to know the meaning of 'battledore and shuttlecock' (line 46) or be familiar with 'a china teapot' and so these references are omitted from the reading. Nick substitutes a potentially problematic word 'prowling' for 'came along' (line 35) and checks that the children know the word 'concrete' (line 39) which had been discussed on the previous page and would have significance later in the story.

These children had spent a year in the nursery and their responses, questions and commentaries demonstrate that many of them seem to have internalised the expectations for engaging in a dialogue and are participating readily, although there are still some who remain silent. They also need less reminding than the younger children of how to engage in appropriate behaviour.

### Taking meaning from a picture book

Nick is guiding the children to make sense of the pictures by drawing their attention to features that will help them to understand the story. – *Look here's the pig. Looking over the wall, can you see?* (lines 22-24); reinforcing children's responses when they do this independently. *That looks like a garden doesn't it Kadeisha, you're right* (line 55-57).

The duality of picture books can make demands on the reader to read the words through the pictures and the pictures through the words to understand the layers of meaning . Nick moves beyond labelling to help the children understand the text by relating the pictures to the immediate text and the overall narrative and by drawing on their knowledge of the world to make sense of the story. *Can you guess what he said?* (lines 59-61).

Nick's focus is on guiding the children to understand sequences of action, cause and effect, and the relationship between characters and actions. He spends some time on the page that shows the wolves innocently playing while the pig lurks menacingly in the background, watching his prey. He is involved in a complex strategy that requires children to read beyond the words to predict what they think is going to happen and draw inferences from the text: *What do you think happens next?* (line 6). Leyton's contribution at the end of the extract, *That will make the pig scared* (line 75), demonstrates that he is already beginning to empathise with characters and identify how they are feeling. This is an aspect of reading that these children will be expected to have grasped in their Primary schools, as the following National Curriculum assessment criteria show:

In responding to a range of texts, pupils show understanding of significant ideas, themes, events and characters, *beginning to use inference and deduction* (my italics).They refer to the text when explaining their views. They locate and use ideas and information. (DfEE/QCA 1999:56)

### Learning how to feel

Nick, acting as an intermediary between the children and the text, communicates in several ways at once, by questioning, pointing and inviting children to predict. He supports the children's understanding of the verbal information in the text and the visual information in the pictures but he is doing more than that.

Firstly, he inserts his own comments on the text to help the children's understanding and show how they might feel about an event or character. *And there he is – oh my goodness – shall we read on and find out what happened?* (lines 26-28). The children are already excited about the pig staring over the wall and Nick's comments shows his agreement that this is something to be worried about.

Secondly, he uses prosodic cues such as stress, tone, volume, speed and rhythm to help the children interpret the author's intended effect on the reader. For example, line 35 *the Big Bad Pig* is read with deliberate emphasis and more slowly than the rest of the passage, accompanied by a frown and a change of posture and he stresses the first syllable of each word to emphasise that this behaviour should be interpreted as frightening. In lines 62-64 Nick reads *Little frightened wolves, can I come in?* in a light-hearted, rhythmic sing-song voice, to signal to the children that the bad pig is employing subterfuge by pretending to be friendly so that he can gain entry to the wolves' house.

By using paralinguistic features – which are evident throughout the whole story reading episode – Nick is indicating that the words have to be interrogated if their polysemic nature is to be understood. The children are learning where to look for signals that will help them interpret the layers of meaning of the text, but in doing so they are also learning what is appropriate to think and to feel in the culture. Nick is using talk and other cues in specific ways to help them understand the story and he is also helping to shape their responses by suggesting interpretations and modelling feelings about a character or an event which reflect a particular set of values.

The children are also being guided into a way of reading and taking meaning from a picture book that is seen as valuable within the culture of school literacy. The pattern of the interaction is dialogic: questions are asked and answered and children are encouraged to take turns. They are co-construct-ing the story with Nick. Reading is a collaborative venture, a social experience and a negotiation between the adult and children who are encouraged to be actively involved in the process. Specific norms, attitudes and values are being reinforced in the story reading event. It is never as simple as just sharing a book with children. A sociocultural view will always connect the literacy event (group story reading in school) with the literacy practices (the be-haviour, expectations and attitudes expected in that context). The children are apprenticed into the culture of school literacy through co-constructing meaning in the ZPD. It is easy to see this as a normal or natural way of reading because it is so pervasive but, as noted earlier, school literacy is just one form. It may well reflect ways of reading in some homes but will be unfamiliar in others.

Picture books such as this are used extensively in nurseries and schools to give a visual focus that will help children understand key aspects of a story. However, the texts themselves are not neutral but inherently ideological in either explicit or more often implicit ways (Hollindale, 1992). As we saw, Nick is helping the children to apply certain values to the characters in the story. The idea of a story about pigs which appears unproblematic to the staff, may be something that is distasteful for some of these young children and un-acceptable to their families on religious grounds. But this tension between different cultural norms and values is not mentioned or explicitly signalled and these children have to make sense of it as best they can, and on their own.

## Discontinuities between home and school

The gap between the practices and expectations of home and school can create problems for some children. Heath's study found that each of the three communities had distinctive ways of using and taking meaning from texts and socialising their children into an understanding of literacy. Her work showed the congruencies and discontinuities between home, community and school based literacy practices and the differential impact for the chil-dren's success at school.

Denny Taylor and Cathe Dorsey-Gaines (1988) and, more recently, Catherine Compton-Lilly (2003) and Rebecca Rogers (2003) have focused on the literacy practices of urban families living in poverty and shown how print and other forms of representation were used proficiently in day to day activities for real purposes. Yet the children from these families were considered to have prob-lems with literacy at school and were the subject of deficit views and often assigned to special compensatory programmes.

## Making connections between home and school

Eve Gregory (2001, 2007) studied young bilingual children at home with their families and at school. She highlighted the strengths they brought to school and challenged the parent-child dyad as the dominant model of literacy learning. She demonstrated how older children made use of a combination of strategies and knowledge derived from home and school contexts to scaffold the literacy learning of their younger siblings. Gregory's work, mostly with the Bangladeshi-British community, showed how these children drew on their cultural and linguistic knowledge to make their own meanings.

Charmian Kenner's (2000, 2004) work with young bilingual children revealed what she termed their simultaneous 'literacy worlds' as they participated in family literacy activities in their home languages. She observed the children in school and was instrumental in facilitating opportunities for them to reveal and extend that knowledge, for example to develop an understanding of how to write in Gujerati or represent the Arabic alphabet. The children's agency in drawing on their cultural and literacy worlds and connecting what they knew from home with what they were learning in school in English led Kenner to believe that they experienced these worlds simultaneously rather than separately. She demonstrated how six year olds who were becoming biliterate used graphic symbols to make connections across writing systems. Her work has been significant in revealing how such young children understand the differences between their literacy worlds but also actively make connections and synthesise them.

A central premise of this book is that children who are learning a new language must have access to their first language so their knowledge and understanding can continue to develop, rather than be restricted by a language which is still emerging (Cummins, 2000; Skutnabb-Kangas, 2000).

## Literacy and the third space

This rest of the book examines the literacy experiences of a group of three and four year olds who attended one urban nursery and the extent to which they appeared to integrate their different worlds of home and school. In the story reading example discussed earlier, all the children brought their own experience of literacy from home to the new reading situation. They would be looking for links between this new way of reading and what they already know from home. Later, through their play, they might draw on what they have learned from school about literacy in combination with what they know from home. This is the 'third space': it is not immediately visible and will be different for each child. Chris Gutiérrez and colleagues (2000) argue that third space theory uncovers the complexities involved in a learning environment as learners draw on familiar cultural resources in unfamiliar institutionalised settings. They characterised the third space as the merging of the first space, typically the funds of knowledge developed in the community and second space, the more formalised knowledge of institutions such as schools. The third space, they argue, is a place where ways of knowing, understanding, behaving and feeling in different contexts can meet to produce potentially productive results.

Elizabeth Birr Moje and her colleagues (2004) suggest that the third space is relevant to education in three different ways . Knowledge and experience in the first space of home can

- provide a bridge to the new ways of learning in school
- be used in combination with school knowledge as an approach to solving a problem or gaining new understanding
- be merged with school knowledge to create new hybrid practices and knowledge.

Definitions of the third space are important for this book because they provide a theoretical frame for interpreting young children's understanding of literacy. The following chapters aim to capture the distinctive ways in which the six children made sense of their new experiences in the nursery and drew on their knowledge of contexts, languages, texts, practices and values from home to create a metaphorical third space that allowed them to link the two. These relate principally to the first and second categories highlighted by Moje and colleagues. The final category is exemplified in the next chapter by the mother of one of the children.

# 3

## Kabir: crossing boundaries between languages and cultures

*Kabir enters the nursery holding his father's hand. He smiles broadly in response to greetings from the staff and goes straight to the computer where he explains to his father in Sylheti that he needs a pen so that he can write his name on the computer list. He waves goodbye and sits down next to his friend Daniel who has already selected the menu.*

Kabir lives with his parents and two sisters Halima (8) and Jakia (5). His mother Sabina was born in the UK to parents who had recently arrived from Bangladesh, and was the first member of her family to go to school here. The family spoke Sylheti-Bengali at home and she learned English at school. She was taught Bengali and Arabic by her father and at the Mosque school she attended in the evenings. When she finished her GCSEs Sabina left school to get married and now works as a teaching assistant in a local primary school. Kabir's father was educated in the Sylhet area of Bangladesh and went on to study law. When he came to the UK he worked as a waiter in the evenings in the local restaurant. He is not yet a confident speaker of English and Sabina translates for him as we speak about Kabir.

### Kabir's literacy experiences
Kabir's experience of literacy within the family is rich and varied. He sees his elder sister, Halima learning to read and write Bengali with their father, using books brought from Mosque school or bought in the local shops. The children also read to their mother and to each other from the books in English they bring home from school. The three children draw and write together in their play, using Bengali and English scripts which they see around them. Their father writes and receives letters from their extended family in Bangladesh

27

and he reads newspapers in Bengali. They see Bengali in the local shops, on signs in the street and in the books they buy locally. They see English in books brought home from school and from the book club where Sabina buys books for Halima. English is on display on the billboards outside their home and on the children's TV channel which they watch regularly.

### Reading a religious text

Sabina formally supports Kabir's literacy learning in two main ways. Firstly she introduces him to reading that has religious significance.

> I'm teaching him Arabic because ehm, that's more important because we believe our deeds are what go with us. So to me it's very important that he learns to read in Arabic. And one day hopefully he'll read the Qur'an like my eldest daughter Halima does.

Sabina underlines the significance of this activity for the family's identity as Muslims. She has made a conscious decision to prioritise the teaching of Arabic rather than Bengali to the younger children, because of its religious significance.

> Everything we read in Arabic has a meaning, an Islamic meaning.

It is likely that Kabir is following in the footsteps of his older sisters and is already internalising the religious significance the text and the language has for his family and community and the potential to transfer meanings from the page into life. Sabina told me:

> Well, I tell Jakia that she has to learn how to read anything in Arabic. Obviously I've told her and she knows that ... I don't know, she just knows that this is important.

> We say it word for word. That's right. And you have to say it in an accurate way. I can't make up a word. I can't add anything or take out anything. It has to be said exactly the way we have been taught for many many hundred years.

Sabina explains that the strategies for reading the text are linked to its historic and religious significance and to shared beliefs. The clearly defined roles of adult and children in observing, reciting and practising no doubt help the children to understand this religious and cultural tradition too.

### Reading a picture book

When Kabir brings books home from nursery, Sabina supports his literacy learning in a different way. She might read to him or she might let him talk about the pictures. This too is an important time for the family but the purposes are quite different. Sabina explains:

> He likes to just look through the pictures. But I let him do it because I think it's important that he enjoys the book. If he knows that he has to sit and read it to me, I don't think he'd ever go through a book.

Here the importance is centred on the enjoyment of the activity and Kabir's motivation to continue with it. There is no deep personal significance in the message of the text or of its value to the family

That the process differs in the two examples illuminates a different set of expectations about the nature of reading. Sabina talks about the strategies she and Kabir use:

> He reads a lot of words from memory. He makes up his own story and I leave it. I don't try to correct him because it's nice. It's nice that my son can use his imagination, make up words. So I let him read what he wants to read and then I sit back and read it to him and then I sort of say the words and get him to point.

When reading a storybook she adopts a different approach to when they are reading the religious text. She gives Kabir free reign to use his imagination but before the encounter is completed she attends to the detail by reading the story accurately and asking him to point to the words.

## The third space

Sabina's own experience of learning the Qur'an was in the traditional way: when she was a child she sat on the floor with the other children repeating the text prompted by her father or teacher who maintained the formality of both the process of repetition and the relationship between adult and learner. But she has decided to employ a new approach based on her experience of being a teaching assistant and of a television programme she watched which asserted that children learn language best when they do not realise they are learning. She believes that children learn through use of praise in an informal way and explains her strategy for encouraging her two younger children to recite from the sacred text as she reads

> She sits here next to me (*demonstrates in the crook of her arm*) and she knows she gets my full attention. Then I say well done and I give her a kiss or something. She likes being praised a lot. She will say 'I'm a clever girl'. And then (Kabir) will say 'I'm a clever boy' and he comes up to me. But I don't say come here and sit down and read it because he will never learn like that and he'll lose interest.

She is providing Kabir and his siblings with a model of hybridised behaviour undertaken every day in the course of a routine but highly significant family activity.

In chapter 2 we saw how the third space has been characterised as the development of new forms of learning that arise from the combination of experiences from different contexts. It is helpful as a tool for showing how people who are at the intersection of different discourses can draw on that knowledge and experience to create new hybridised ways of knowing and doing. Sabina is creating a third space by drawing on practices that are integral to her simultaneous literacy worlds (Kenner, 2004). Whilst retaining traditional community strategies of recitation and memorisation, she draws on the informality of the western primary school discourse to teach the Qur'an by using motivating strategies and deliberate use of praise.

This new way of learning is not represented within either the space of community or of school learning but forms a new practice drawing on cultural resources from both sites. Sabina is providing her children with a model of how to create a third space and move between different literate identities.

## Kabir at school

Kabir is learning about literacy in Bengali, Arabic and English from a close and loving connection with family members mediated through the family language, Sylheti-Bengali. At nursery he is beginning to use English as the medium for learning. In term 1 a nursery nurse consulted the list of key phrases in Sylheti, written phonetically for the staff who don't speak it. She asks Kabir if he is alright, to which he replies 'yes' in English, with a smile. At the same time as learning when to use Sylheti-Bengali or English in the nursery, he also made decisions about which reading strategy to draw on. In the following example from his first term in the nursery, he is applying familiar practices of watching, listening and repeating that he engages in at home.

### Drawing on familiar strategies for learning

It is small group story time, for the youngest children. Linda the nursery nurse is reading *Dear Zoo*. Each child has their own copy and Linda invites them to link the language of the story with the written text and to be actively involved by joining in and lifting the flap to reveal the animal underneath. Kabir, who is new to the nursery at this stage, copies Linda and the other children, choosing to focus on them rather than looking at the pictures in the book. He repeats key words, such as the name of an animal or even a whole line, quietly, just slightly behind everyone else. When he turns to the wrong page, he checks and confidently moves it back until he is at the same page as everyone else.

A few weeks later, while listening to the nursery teacher read *Whatever Next* to a small group at the end of the morning, Kabir was chosen to hold a star. He sat staring ahead, sometimes yawning and not particularly involved. Later that day, listening to *The Gingerbread Man,* he leant on another child, trying unsuccessfully to get his attention and then sitting with his hands on his cheeks and then over his eyes. But once Linda asked *What song do you think the Gingerbread man sang?* he sat up and listened to the repetitive refrain, smiling as the children sang *Run, run as fast as you can,* confidently joining in with the final line *and you can't catch me.*

This pattern of carefully watching and following the lead from other children continued for some months during small and large group story time. For Kabir it was an important strategy for learning English and for finding his way around books and stories. At this time, Kabir was often to be found with head-phones on, listening to taped stories in Bengali and English, holding the book, nodding his head silently to the music that accompanied them. Later he would join in with key phrases from the reading, turning the pages at the appropriate time.

### *Learning to give meaning to text*

As Kabir became accustomed to the nursery and more confident in speaking English he assumed more autonomy and began to make more deliberate choices about how to spend his time. In term 2 he shared an information book *Amazing Lizards* with two older Bangladeshi-British boys in an encounter that was to be often repeated with different books. The medium was English but the scope of their conversations was far wider:

The children are poring over a picture of a lizard in the book:

| | |
|---|---|
| Ch 1 | It's gonna bite you that's why I don't like that one |
| Ch 2 | Once I saw a scary one in the bathroom. My brother said I can't hold it it gonna bite him |
| Ch1 | I saw a frog in the bathroom and my aunty throwed it outside and I saw another one under the bed |
| K: | Don't like it it's gonna bite |
| Ch 2 | The big spiders gonna fight with your spider I'm going to get a big one or a little one |

K:        A little one

Ch 2     My spider's going to fight your spider. It's going to pick you up so high and put you in a cage and I'm gonna to send a crocodile to eat you up.

The children are making links with their lives in England and Bangladesh. But they are also using the book as the basis for storytelling which draws on elements of competition, bravado and playful hostility. The two older boys are modelling how a book can be a medium for drawing on resources from different cultural worlds and demonstrating to four year old Kabir the cultural flexibility that characterises the process of learning for young bilingual, bicultural children.

Male solidarity as a way into literacy appeared more frequently in Kabir's repertoire over time as he engaged in various activities with other boys. They made competitive exchanges about, for example, who knew the most letters of the alphabet, who could turn the pages of a book more quickly and who was going to get a space rocket that most resembled the picture in the book. Space rockets featured strongly in the boys' role-play, construction, drawing and mark-making.

When looking at picture books on other occasions the boys exchanged experiences about, for example, playing Batman in Bangladesh, being bitten by a spider there or being chased by a snake. When Kabir had been in the nursery for one term, a nursery teacher, Cathy overheard him talking to his friend Fahim in Sylheti, and asked Kabir if he was going to Bangladesh. To which he replied:

> I'm going to my home in my home. And you're going to Fahim Bangladesh and I'm going to go in my Bangladesh and he is going Fahim going to go home.

Such conversations reveal the simultaneous worlds that Kabir inhabits and about which he finds expression with other children. Cathy's question gave him an opportunity to reveal an important insight into his identity which she and the rest of the staff might not otherwise have accessed.

### Kabir's interest in media technology and story

By his third term, Kabir had a deep interest in the computer and had developed proficiency in manipulating the mouse for his own purposes, selecting and reselecting the required programme by clicking on the title from the menu *The Enormous Turnip* or *The Three Billy Goats Gruff*, replaying films recorded in the nursery and games involving recognising and clicking on a range of icons and other symbols. He could click on the arrow to move to the next or the previous page, join in with the dialogue and sing along with the accompanying music. Such noticeable interest in screen texts prompted the nursery teacher, Nick to remark that Kabir was going to become a film director.

The family did not have a computer at home, but one day Kabir's father showed me how his son had expertly used the remote control to play games on Sky TV and had used a bottle top as a camera, making his family pose for a photograph. Kabir seemed to be able to make the leap to multimedia through a combination of interest in screen texts, watching and listening to other children and trial and error during repeated interactions with favourite computer programmes. His comment to his friend Amir that the 'play' button meant 'go' suggests he was not decoding the word but using his knowledge of its function.

Kabir's engagement with literacy was for his own purposes, for pleasure and as a means of signalling solidarity with a group of other boys, whose activities he first watched from the periphery. He showed concentration and involvement when engaged in self chosen activities, as for example in his drawing and mark making. One day, over a twenty five minute period and with meticulous precision, he created a picture using a fine tipped pen, often pausing before deciding what to draw next. When I asked about his picture, he told me it was 'the world, my dad, a space rocket and some steps' and proceeded to represent this by a cluster of letters in the right hand corner (see Figure 3.1).

By term 3 Kabir could find his own name card and had learnt to recognise the written names of other children in the class too. He told me he could read 'Nadia' because he knew *N,a,d. . .* When asked to hold up the name cards for children to go to lunch, he would look at the card and hold it in the direction of the appropriate child, although he was still too shy to name them.

Kabir was less likely to be involved when literacy activities were teacher initiated such as group storytime. When invited to share a text with an adult he would reluctantly recite from memory but would not respond to invitations to talk about the book. His growing enjoyment of story, however, was evident through his interest in the computer. The nursery teacher frequently filmed storytime role play episodes, and these would be put on the computer for general consumption. These were favourites for Kabir, as were taped books in English and Bengali. His view of story as entertainment as well as his familiarity with narrative conventions began to grow – as we can see when Kabir and three other children were sitting round a table eating the star shaped jam sandwiches they had just made and he said:

Shall I tell you a story yeh
First there was a monster yeh
He ate the moon up
Now he's sick
He's gone to bed.

The nursery theme at the time was Space, with a particular focus on *Whatever Next?* a story about a bear who visits the moon. Some children, guided by the nursery teacher, had been looking at the NASA website. It is likely that Kabir's story, told to entertain the audience while they ate their 'space sandwiches', was inspired by the factual and fictional focus on the moon and space.

## Linking home and school: the third space

When he entered the nursery, Kabir's literate identity was bound by the strategies, attitudes and the texts which were integral to the language and culture of his home and community. As we have seen, he could draw on that knowledge but he also developed new understandings as he became more familiar with the nursery. He clearly felt secure with the prevalence of story and narrative as a medium for learning because of his involvement with television and film at home and his experiences of sharing a book with his mother. He built on his interest in screen texts and developed his dexterity at using the TV remote control to help him manipulate the computer mouse and engage with multimedia texts, most often making sense of the print and other symbols on the screen in the company of his male friends.

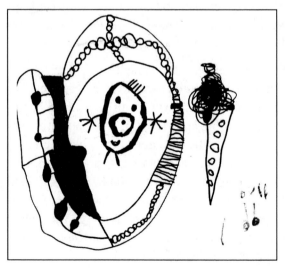

**Figure 3.1 Kabir's picture. The world, my dad, a space rocket and some steps**

His experiences at home with his sisters had prepared him for the nursery discourse of play-based learning and he felt comfortable making choices and engaging in activities both independently and as part of a group. His involvement in their more formal aspects of reading and writing either as observer or participant had also enabled him to acquire a familiarity with Bengali and English scripts, although interestingly English became visible in his mark making, but not Bengali.

However, there were aspects of his home literacy learning that were not congruent with the nursery. Although Bengali was evident in the nursery in dual language books in the book area and in labels and signs and notices for parents, Arabic was not represented as readily. Yet this was the language of texts that were read every day at home and treated with such respect and reverence. Also at home, each language was attached to a different text or genre, whereas this was not the case in the nursery. Kabir had to learn which aspects of his home discourse fitted with the nursery and which parts were for the family and community context.

Kabir's experience reinforces the view that literacy practices involve ideological models and as such cannot be separated from wider cultural and power structures. Sabina's strong conviction about the moral value and religious significance of reading in Arabic is a product of her family's historical and cultural roots; it is a driving force in their life and yet it is of no account in the secular world Kabir encounters in school.

Nonetheless Kabir is experiencing more than one teaching and learning strategy at home and at nursery. His 'simultaneous worlds' enable him to engage in different sorts of literacy, each with distinctive behaviours values and roles. From such events as those described above, Kabir is learning about different expectations and definitions of literacy as well as the behaviours that surround literacy in different contexts.

However, Kabir also appeared to develop strategies and relationships that enabled him to draw on his bicultural experience and the new opportunities for literacy learning offered by the nursery environment. Book sharing and computer-based sessions with other boys featured strongly in his repertoire of activities and offered a new relationship with texts and meaning-making and gave him pleasure and satisfaction. Kabir, in the company of other bilingual, bicultural children, appeared to have created a third space for literacy learning where the worlds of home and school could meet.

# 4

## Michelle: 'Can someone pass the yellow ?'
## Talk, literacy and being a girl

*Michelle arrives at nursery with her older sister and confidently joins a group of girls who are sitting with the nursery teacher making their own 'Dear Zoo' books. Michelle begins her book too, telling everyone that she will give it to her sister as a birthday present.*

Michelle lives with her mother Jacintha and her sister Shereen and is part of a close extended family network. Jacintha was born in Jamaica and came to England when she was five. Although she enjoyed primary school, she had a negative experience of secondary education because of her undetected dyslexia which left her feeling confused, angry and disillusioned with school and the education system. She left school with no qualifications but decided to further her own education by attending evening classes in computing, spelling and English grammar. Still embarrassed and traumatised by her experience, she talks about the difficulties of seeking help:

> The first time, I went to the Centre in the evening cos I didn't want no-one to see me and the funny thing is, I stayed outside for about half and hour, I didn't want to go in and I walked away. And the next day I thought right, I'm going in there.

Jacintha now works in a library. Her experience when she was a teenager and her self-identification as a person with literacy problems has had an impact on her views about education and motherhood:

> And that's when I thought to myself I wouldn't want Michelle or Shereen to be like that. I'd rather give as much help because I didn't have much help – I like to give them as much help as I possibly can and if it means starting at an early age then that is what I will do.

Who says you have to wait until you're five years old before they can start reading and writing. I think in the West Indies they start earlier anyway and they can't believe that school starts at that age.

## Michelle's literacy experiences

Michelle's sister Shereen is fourteen years older than she is and a frequent recipient of the letters and cards she creates in the nursery. Jacintha says she *looks up to her sister. She wants to wear her shoes and carry bags like her and do everything Shereen does.*

She sees her mum reading *Now* magazine and *The Voice,* and they visit the library regularly. Jacintha likes books about people's lives, *what actually happened to that person, what they went through, how did they deal with it and how they are now.*

Michelle is read to by both Jacintha and Shereen and she will not go to bed without a story. Jacintha says that Michelle can read favourite stories from memory: *She's not looking at the words but she remembers the pictures and how the story goes.* Recently she has begun to point at words and ask what they say. She is also encouraged to talk about the messages in the book and think about the connections with her own life. A book from the library they had been reading recently was about looking after a puppy and taking it to the vet for an injection. Michelle was puzzled by the idea of an injection and Jacintha explained that Michelle also needed to have vaccinations as a baby.

Michelle watches interactive children's programmes on Sky TV. She especially enjoys the Disney children's channel, which often has games and puzzles and singing and clapping rhymes she joins in with, encouraged by Shereen. They also dance together to the music. Recently she has been watching a children's cartoon about how to find your way using a map and Jacintha has recorded it so that she can watch it again.

Even with like Tweenies. They have a lot of numbers and counting and alphabet that helps them as well because it's all singing and dancing and she likes it.

The focus is on Michelle's enjoyment and the pleasure of being engaged in joint activity but has the serious purpose of preparing her for what she will experience in school.

Michelle is at the centre of a close family of women. She has four aunties as role models as well as her mother and sister. According to her mother, she is a *girlie girl* and *surrounded by lots of females* and this seems to be an important focus for her reading and writing activities. Similarly in the nursery, as we shall see, most of her spontaneous literacy activity is connected with her identity as a girl.

At home, Jacintha's understanding of learning to read and write perhaps reflects her own early experiences. She encourages Michelle to write notes and letters to family members and learn to write their names accurately.

> She has problems with Aunty Rose she can't do Rose. It's the Rs and the Os. But she asks me and she tries to do it. And sometimes 'Let me show you' 'Noooo'. The thing with Michelle is she has to try...she has to try to do it for herself and if she can't do it then she'll ask for your help.

She emphasises the importance of making the enormous task of becoming literate manageable for Michelle.

> She gets paper after paper and she will just sit there and she will write. She says write aunty Jenny, write aunty Rose, write aunty Beverley. And I'm writing all the names down and I say you can't remember all of them, let's concentrate on two first. Get to know that first and then we can go back to it.

Jacintha's support for Michelle's literacy learning involves helping her learn sequentially, developing skills such as letter formation and learning the alphabet as well as encouraging her independence. But through this self regulated activity Michelle is also learning about written language. She is beginning to learn that the groups of letters that represent her name and those of her close family are consistent and unvarying. She will also come to know that these groups of letters stand for herself, her mum or her aunties and can conjure up in her mind what they look like, how they feel, how they laugh or walk and behave towards her. She is beginning to understand that written language is a symbolic system.

## Michelle at nursery

At nursery, Michelle demonstrated her knowledge of the more technical aspects of literacy and showed pride in accuracy and independent achievement. In term 2 she was engaged in a puzzle based on *Spot The Dog*. Each piece says *Spot has lost his bone* and matches with a corresponding one *Is it under the cushion? Is it in the drawer?* etc. She picks out *No* and *Yes* to complete each line. Seeing me writing, she tells me there are two Ms in mummy and that she knows because her sister told her!

On another occasion she expertly pegged a piece of paper on the painting easel, did a drawing and wrote both her name and her sister's. I asked what her drawing was about and she told me, *I've got lots of family. That's how you spell my sister's name, two 'e's* (pointing). She then added an 'i'. *She's got an 'i' in it.* Then she put an 'i' in her own name.

Although the alphabet is not explicitly taught in the nursery, there is an alphabetic chart of children's names on display and plastic letters and alphabet software are available as resources for children's play. Michelle has an interest brought from home in choosing, naming and forming letters accurately to represent names which, she has learned, are symbolic representations for important people in her life. However, she had not yet fully grasped the concept of written language. For example, one day, in response to hearing the *Three Billy Goats Gruff* read aloud, she made her own picture, accompanied by strings of letters, and told me that she had drawn the bridge, the water, *the words* and the sun.

*That went over the hill and down there and the troll was trying to gobble them up. And they was trying to eat the green grass and they was trying to get over the bridge round and round and round.'*

**Figure 4.1 Retelling The Three Billy Goats Gruff in words and pictures**

*The Three Billy Goats Gruff* remained a favourite story at nursery for several weeks as Michelle drew, role played and shared the book with her friends and listened to it on tape. She often read books to other children, using a combination of picture clues and memory. In the example in figure 4.1, spontaneously produced during the *Three Billy Goats Gruff* period, Michelle is retelling part of the story. She is representing the action in her picture to carry the story and as a stimulus for the words. She is also following narrative conventions and adopting story language. Her interest in names can be seen in the letter shapes she uses to represent her message.

Michelle's familiarity with and interest in stories was evident in her enthusiasm for group story, where, secure with the pattern of question, response, feedback from reading with her sister and mother at home, she responded confidently to adult enquiries, showing her own interpretation of the story.

Nick, the nursery teacher is reading a story to a group of children, including Michelle.

| Nick | Yesterday we read *The Elephant and the Bad Baby* |
| | Do you remember how the story started? |
| Michelle | He found a friend |
| Nick | Yes, he found a friend. |

The children are listening to Linda, the nursery nurse read *You'll Soon Grow Into Them Titch.*

| Linda | Why do you think the trousers didn't fit Titch? |
| Michelle | Cos he's a children |
| Linda | That's right he was too small for them. |

One of Michelle's favourite books was *So Much*, a story about the warmth of family life as members of an extended African-Caribbean family come to visit the baby and his parents. In the narrative and dialogue are resonances of the Creole that Michelle would hear at family gatherings with her mother, aunties and grandparents.

By term 3 Michelle could manipulate the computer mouse expertly, directing it to the menu for a list of stories, games and other programs. She said aloud *the Tortoise and the Hare* as she pressed the Play button and she listened to the narrative while watching the animation, concentrating on the screen, mouse in hand. She joined in with the dialogue as she clicked on the characters, who moved as they spoke. She moved the cursor to the icon to repeat the story and then to *Yes* in response to *Are you sure you want to quit?* She could deliberately include music and this appeared to play an important part in her enjoyment. She could also recognise a range of different icons: for example, she could make the sun come up by clicking on the yellow circle. On another occasion, at the end of watching an animation of *Ruff's Bone*, she had to make a choice between *listen to the music* or *start again*. She chose to listen to the music twice more and on the final time went back and replayed the whole story.

Michelle was firmly in control throughout the navigation of these multimedia stories and games, interpreting and manipulating the symbols on the screen. The availability of sound, colour and moving image contributed to her overall understanding of the meaning and added an extra perspective that would not have been present through print alone.

### Linking home and school: the third space

In the nursery, Michelle's agency and intention were apparent. She spoke with confident authority and was a leading member of a group of girls who were often to be found mark making, drawing and cutting out letters, cards and homemade books, while engaged in conversations that were mainly concerned with organising and making sense of their world. The following extract, which is typical of many conversations, showed how far Michelle's orientations to literacy in the nursery were rooted in her home culture:

Michelle, Latifah and Katy are making birthday cards:

| | |
|---|---|
| Michelle | I'm making a silly girl |
| Latifah | No, Look it's got hair |
| Michelle | You have two bunches like I have it (referring to the drawing) |
| Latifah | Have I Michelle? |
| Michelle | No today you haven't plaits (referring to Latifah's hair) |
| Latifah | You got two plaits. |
| Katy | Have you got three plaits? |
| Michelle | I've got two plaits. This one's got plaits. I'm gonna take this one home. This one's for my Barbie. |
| Latifah | I'm doing a girl on it |
| Michelle | A purple girl and a purple top |

| | |
|---|---|
| Katy | The one on the tummy |
| Michelle | Katy you don't have to moan about it. I'm talking to you. When I talk to you you don't just cry when I'm talking |
| Latifah | I've got a girl in a top |
| Michelle | You can't be like a baby. Babies cry, not big girls. |

The girls were busy and involved in this activity. Michelle was expertly choosing colours and drawing on the front of the card. Later she would include letter shapes. The others were already embarking on their message inside. The conversation related to a range of stereotypically female preoccupations, mostly concerned with appearance. The children were using language to mediate their experience. Latifah is also of Caribbean heritage and both girls usually had their hair in plaits or cane row. Aware no doubt of their shared ethnicity, Latifah asked a question about her hair, sounding confident that Michelle would know the answer. Home life was their main focus and concern, including the parental voice, which was rehearsed by Michelle at the end of the sequence and was a reminder to the others of how 'big girls' behave.

As the children drew and wrote, they explored issues of female identity from within their own world, often with some competitiveness and rivalry. Their conversations related to familiar themes such as 'bathing babies', 'doing the washing', 'what mummies say' and 'birthday parties'. These collaborative mark making occasions appeared to be closely bound up with explicitly talking about home experiences and concerns, echoing the voices of important people in their lives.

The girls also incorporated the familiar cultural resources of songs, film and TV into their play. When Michelle, engaged in the familiar practices of drawing and writing, was telling the girls about *Beauty and the Beast* which she had seen on TV, she remembered the refrain *when your dreams come* true, which she wanted to put next to her picture.

One day the three friends all came to nursery with writing on their tee shirts. They spent time, reading and comparing them. Michelle had *Army Girl* on hers, Latifah had *Cheeky Girls* and Latifah had *37*. Another time, Michelle and her friend Katy experimented with new roles as teenage girls, drawing the Cheeky Girls and singing *We Are The Cheeky Girls*, stopping to copy the actions of the original singers they had seen on TV.

Michelle and her friends expressed their own identities and preoccupations through mark making and the talk that surrounded it. The unity of the group was revealed by remarks such *can someone pass me the yellow* and *has anyone got a pen* which related to the collaborative nature of the activity at hand. But the most immediate and pressing concern seemed to be to investigate and compare the roles and relationships of females:

Michelle and Molly are making a book about their mums:

> Michelle:     My daddy's got a mum. See my mum she's got a dress on, she's going out. She looks at the mirror and does this face (makes a face).

Texts produced during these activities were books, letters, cards, invitations as well as those grounded in real life experiences such 'my list for Asda'; 'what do you want from the chip shop' and 'my homework'. The children seemed to be talking, drawing, singing and playing their way into literacy through the creation of self initiated texts that were the meeting point for a wealth of knowledge from home.

Anne Haas Dyson (2003) has spent many years observing how young children incorporate their knowledge of their own worlds and particularly popular culture in creating their own texts. She focused on a small group of first grade African American children as they 'appropriated' their knowledge from pop songs, jingles, cartoons, superheroes, sports icons, video games with teacher sanctioned texts in school. Michelle and her friends were also sharing and comparing their identities from home and beginning to represent these preoccupations in their mark making, shown in Figure 4.2. But the most important matter seemed to be the talk that surrounded it.

There were commonalities between Michelle's literacy experiences in the first space of home and the second space of the nursery. She was familiar with story and the discussion that surrounded it; she was comfortable with play based learning and the expectation of independence in initiating self chosen activities. She effortlessly seemed to incorporate new school related forms of literacy such as book-making, writing registers and large group stories into her repertoire. She could draw on a range of texts and modes of representation and was familiar with the world of popular culture as a stimulus for her reading and mark making.

Although the nursery's developmental philosophy did not emphasise accurate representation or practising the letters of the alphabet, Michelle seemed comfortable with this despite her preoccupations at home. She took pleasure in her own competence, using literacy for her own purposes, to connect with others at home and school, integrating it into a special kind of personally meaningful language play, based on real life. This was the third space where Michelle appeared to locate herself between the worlds of home and school.

Opportunities to engage with literacy in the nursery offered a context for Michelle to collaboratively reflect on the familiar world of home and to examine and revisit experiences and expectations. Michelle operated confidently and happily within the nursery, responding positively to adult direction while always coming back to her own preoccupations.

# 5

## Sadia: interpreting the rules
## for literacy learning

*Sadia and her father arrive at nursery and she sits down at a table that is laid out with a card matching activity. She whispers to him in Sylheti and they move to another table where there are coloured pegs to be put in sequence. She sits on her own, still with her coat and hat on, proficiently placing the pegs in the base according to their colour.*

Sadia's mother and father came to the UK from Bangladesh ten years ago. They went to school in the same part of Sylhet and, in keeping with tradition in their villages at the time, her father finished formal schooling at fourteen and her mother at eleven. Abdul-Ahad worked as a delivery driver and his wife Tahmina looked after their children: Asia (8), Farhana (7), Sadia (4) and Jabed (2).

The family spoke Sylheti-Bengali at home and Sadia's parents impressed upon their children that it was their own language, the one that connects them to their extended family in Bangladesh. The three older children also learned written Bengali ensuring that they could also communicate with relatives and have access to texts that would strengthen their cultural knowledge and understanding. Sadia's father prioritised the learning of Bengali because he knew the children would learn English at school and that *there are members of staff who can help them to understand if necessary.*

### Sadia's literacy experiences
Each weekend without fail, freed from his early morning weekday schedule, Abdul-Ahad set aside time for family learning. Sadia and her two sisters settled down with him at the kitchen table to learn Arabic and Bengali. He

would have liked to send the two older girls to Mosque school but it was too far away for them to travel. Asia and Farhana are learning to recite the Qur'an under their father's guidance by listening, copying and repeating. Sadia, some years younger than her sisters, is learning the *qa'idah* in stages before she moves on to the Qur'an. She repeated the words after her father, while her sisters practised quietly alongside her. This was an important time for the family, the three children following their father's lead, perfecting their recitation, moving through manageable stages, showing their parents their accomplishments with pride and a sense of achievement.

Sadia's parents also bought books from the local supermarket to help their children learn to read and write Bengali. The older children read these books to their mother while the younger two looked on. Sadia's father taught them the alphabet systematically by spelling out words '*first the letters and how each letter is linked to the next one and then the whole word*'. Sadia enjoyed copying the letters with precision; her sisters were already moving on to writing words.

Sadia's literacy practices were mostly centred on her membership of the Bangladeshi community and her identity as a Muslim. There was a stability about the routine and regularity of literacy at the heart of the family and Sadia's parents were very proud of their children's achievements and their steady progress in learning to recite the Qur'an.

## Learning with siblings

The four children watched television together. *The Teletubbies* was a favourite programme, with each child choosing to be a different character. Sadia joined in with her siblings, repeating the phrases with obvious pleasure. Still just four years old, she was adding reading and writing in English to her repertoire. The older girls brought books home from their primary school which was on the same site as the nursery. Sometimes, Sadia would sit on her own and copy out words from her sisters' books. Recently Asia had been drawing diagrams of fruit and flowers and labelling the different parts and this had become an abiding interest for Sadia too.

The children spoke English to each other and Asia and Farhana would read to Sadia from the books they brought from school. They took it in turns to be in role as teacher, regularly using the books as a basis for playing school with the other children. Eve Gregory (2001, 2007) has shown the significance that playing school with siblings can have for introducing children to school related concepts and practices and new forms of literacy. Rose Drury (2007) has emphasised the importance of this process for very young bilingual children.

Sadia's sisters played an important role in supporting her language and literacy development in Bengali, Arabic and English and introducing her to the more formal aspects of the primary school she would encounter when she moved on from the nursery. It is not surprising that Sadia chose to copy from books alongside her sisters, since this is a valued cultural practice and she engaged in it with her family every weekend as they learned Bengali and Arabic scripts. Sadia's experience of literacy at home was rich and varied and located in close family relationships that bound them to wider family networks and the local Islamic community.

## Sadia at nursery

At nursery Sadia often sat at the first table she went to with her father in the morning and did not move. She kept her coat on and spent long periods watching the other children. She chose puzzles or number related activities, such as sorting or pattern making or occasionally painting and showed no interest in the well stocked mark making area, the beautifully displayed books and tapes, role play or other activities where children were busily engaged in play, many moving between Sylheti-Bengali and English depending on the audience. From her vantage point at the table she would sometimes do nothing more than watch the other children.

Sadia did not appear to be at ease in the nursery environment, as the following observations show:

> Cathy (teacher) sits with Sadia at the bricks table. She quickly puts the bricks in the base in order of size and colour. She nods or shakes her head in response to Pauline's conversation but does not speak and eventually just stares. She goes to throw the bricks very deliberately. Pauline asks her to put them down and she does.

> Sadia is at the painting easel She chooses one colour and paints a number 2 and a number 5, takes off her apron and goes back to sit at the table on her own.

Sadia rarely spoke to children or adults even when personally addressed and the staff put no pressure on her to do so, viewing her non-participation with some amusement as a sign of her determination and spirit but also recognising that some children learning English at school will choose to remain silent while positively assimilating the new language (Krashen,1985; Drury, 2007). Their attempts to encourage her to talk or join in activities with other children were rarely successful.

Sadia watched the other children attentively but did not play alongside them or make any attempt to respond to them when they occasionally spoke to her. She engaged in solitary play, watching but not participating in group activities. In her play alone on the climbing frame outside or with the puzzles and pattern making activities she enjoyed most, she showed dexterity, concentration and a sound understanding of concepts such as ordering and sorting. But she did not choose to engage in the wide range of other activities that were a feature of the well planned nursery environment and so popular with the other children.

At group story time she occasionally joined in with actions songs and would sometimes listen to the story, looking at the pictures, although she did not actively participate in joint meaning making and would remain silent and uninvolved when the adult reading the book stopped to ask children about the story. Sadia rarely spoke about the nursery when she was at home. When she did, it was just before going to sleep, when she would describe what she had seen that day.

## Understanding learning in the nursery

It seems likely that while learning a new language as well as a new culture, Sadia did not understand or feel comfortable with the model of teaching and learning in the nursery: there were few visible teaching strategies and play was conceptualised as work. On one of the few occasions she spoke to me I asked her what she liked doing best at school and she replied 'blowing up balloons'. This suggests that she did not understand what constituted learning in the nursery and did not share the unspoken expectations of the staff about what counted.

Her interest and engagement with mathematical activities may have been because they had clearly defined, observable outcomes whereas the play related activities involving literacy were more open-ended and did not connect to her experiences of learning at home. There was little congruence between the domains of family and school for Sadia and a cultural distance yawned between her expectations and experience and the day-to day life of the nursery. She was unable to understand new meanings in the unfamiliar context of school or grasp the interpretive rules for operating as a member of the nursery. Consequently she was on the periphery.

Sadia's parents were happy with their choice of school and the progress their daughter was making. However, their lack of confidence in speaking English when they brought Sadia to school meant that communication between them and the nursery was sometimes fragile. Some of the staff had developed a construct of the family and misunderstandings sometimes occurred as a result. Sadia's father was sometimes seen as less than co-operative. He had high status in the community as an active and a well respected member of the Mosque but he had low status in the school.

A central element of the nursery staff's philosophy was that children learned best through play in situations that were meaningful to them and where they experienced satisfaction and enjoyment. The environment was planned to maximise opportunities for children to engage in different types of play alone, with others and with adult interaction and support. Staff believed that play supported children's literacy development, in particular through enabling them to develop language, explore narrative and experiment with different forms of representations in familiar contexts. Nigel Hall and Anne Robinson (2003) have written in detail about the ways in which play supports young children's writing development, and the views of the nursery staff were similar.

Sadia's parents were unfamiliar with a play pedagogy. Their view of learning was associated, as we have seen, with adult support and validation and a sense of achievement. Their teaching strategies involved active instruction and although these features were present in nursery practice, they were not immediately apparent or explicitly referred to for parents.

Sadia engaged in role play at home, playing school with her sisters and watching the *Teletubbies* when she would choose to become one of the characters. Yet at nursery the only form of play she engaged in were with activities that provided a concrete challenge. The more spontaneous and open ended forms apparent in the nursery such as role play or free flow play were perhaps not conceived of by Sadia or her parents as being 'school work'. Such tensions between parents' and teachers' views about work and play are not unusual, and early years settings have found their own ways of creating a dialogue about the issue. However it may be that no matter how welcoming the environment, some parents, particularly those who are not confident speakers of English, do not feel comfortable to talk about their expectations. Under these circumstances, if children like Sadia are to reach their potential, it seems necessary for practitioners to interrogate their observations of children to discover what may become barriers to their learning and to be proactive in talking to parents as partners.

## Linking home and school: the third space

For Sadia, the contradictions between the worlds of home and school far out-weighed the congruencies. In the nursery, narrative and story were prioritised as a route into literacy and although Sadia had access to these genres through TV and her sister's school books, this did not appear to be an important con-nection for her. Her pleasure and interest in the Teletubbies at home was not evident in the nursery, although she could sometimes be seen watching re-cordings of nursery role play and storytelling activities from across the room while she sat at her chosen position near the maths activities. At home, her parents said she preferred to join in with her sister's homework tasks in pre-ference to opening the story books she brought from nursery.

For Sadia's family, work and play were demarcated whereas in the nursery there was no such division or expectation. Her lack of involvement in the nursery might be attributed by staff to her developing language skills in English or lack of literacy experience at home. Yet we know that literacy learn-ing with her parents and siblings was a high status activity which they con-nected with their culture, religion and family heritage. But for Sadia, familiar teaching strategies, texts, attitudes and social relationships were not present in the nursery.

Supported by her father, she created a third space that offered opportunities for using her cultural resources and funds of knowledge from home by engag-ing in activities that involved clear rules and results and tangible outcomes. The gap between literacy activities at home and in the nursery seemed too vast for a four year old learning in an unfamiliar language to bridge alone.

What might have helped Sadia to engage with the new world of the nursery and build on her literacy experiences at home? Perhaps if staff could find out more about those experiences and the motivation and involvement that characterised her engagement with them, they could acknowledge and build on them in ways she might recognise. They could for instance, use computer software for her to see and hear Bengali or learn the English alphabet or en-courage her to copy and label. Or they might invite her to bring Bengali texts from home or some of the writing she had done with her father or when play-ing schools. Doing so would recognise her experience and perhaps en-courage other children to share similar experiences that also remained hidden.

# 6

## Jamie: narrative, popular culture and multimodality

*Jamie says goodbye to his mum and brother and after spending a few minutes checking what is going on in the room, decides to sit at a table with a group of other children. He takes a piece of paper and folds it carefully to make a rocket, explaining to Linda the nursery nurse that his nanny showed him how to do it. He shouts '321, blast off' and guides the rocket through the air, saying to Linda that its wings have fallen off and it has died.*

Jamie's family have lived in the same area of East London for four generations. His mother Penny, like her two sisters, attended the primary school Jamie will go to when he leaves nursery. She left secondary school at fifteen and took a job in a local shoe shop. Penny still lives in the family flat with her mother Margaret and Jamie and his brother Michael. She remembers Margaret's involvement in helping her and her sisters prepare for school and how she showed them how to count, using their fingers and toes, and taught them their alphabet and how to write their names.

Margaret has her own memories of reading to the teacher at school:

> You stood one on each side of her and read a page or two from your book. If you got it wrong you were for it. I don't know how she heard half the time because she was often doing something else as well. Going to read to the teacher or the headmistress was always a big thing, you had to get it right.

### Jamie's literacy experiences
When Jamie was a baby he was cared for by his grandfather who has since died. Penny explains:

When he was born my dad looked after him. Mum worked and so did I. They did physical things. He showed him how to use bottle lids, building stuff. He got him plastic tools, hammers and saws. He passed away when Jamie was two and a half. Jamie still asks where he is. He knows he's up in the thunder and when it thunders he's talking to him.

Penny says that her father was a great storyteller, who entertained them with family stories:

He used to tell stories about when he was evacuated and separated from his family. He used to tell stories about when he was a kid, what him and his brothers got up to. When we were having dinner or in the living room we'd say 'tell us about it then'.

Jamie too is steeped in this oral culture. Penny says that *he listens to everything and everything is a story for him* and this love of narrative has extended to televisual texts. He is interested in videos, which his grandmother buys for him and he walks round with his favourites tucked under his arm.

Penny and Margaret devote time and energy to helping Jamie become familiar with the experiences he will have at school. They buy him books from the local shops. His favourites are Disney books, which Penny says he likes to *colour rather than read*. He plays board games with Margaret and they do number puzzles. When they read *Where's Spot?* which Jamie brings home from nursery, she reads through it, lifting the flaps to show him the pictures underneath. Jamie listens *with a serious look on his face and enjoys the pictures*. When Margaret has finished, he looks at them again, turning the pages for himself. He also learned the alphabet. Penny says *we kept on singing it to him but we didn't think he was paying attention, but then he came out with it.*

Jamie also played computer games which drew on his interest in film and popular culture. He sang along to the soundtrack of children's songs while navigating his way through the PlayStation game of *Aladdin* or *Reading Rabbit*. These invite him to click the mouse to identify letters of the alphabet or numbers or shapes hidden in the picture and reward him with stickers and pictures to be coloured in on the screen.

Penny and Margaret chose books and comics that featured favourite characters and stories from TV and films because they know these will interest Jamie. Such experience of intertextuality is likely to enable him to become familiar with different versions and emphases and the transfer of narrative from one medium to another.

### Jamie's interest in multimedia and popular culture

Jamie's interest in technology and popular culture was encouraged by his mother and grandmother, who bought him videos and computer games. Jamie and his brother were adept at using the remote control and could press fast forward, re-play and pause to suit their purposes. Naima Browne (1999) observes how this self regulated behaviour supports children's literacy learning by enabling them to explore narrative and characterisation in more depth and points to the significance of film and video as catalysts for children's dramatic play and storytelling. Margaret sat with the children while they watched videos, replaying sequences, singing along and talking back to the screen, supporting the boys' attempts to re-enact the story, suggesting props they could use and laughing at their antics. Perhaps parallels can be drawn with the warmth, pleasure and security that young children can experience when sharing books with adults. Similarities can also be found with the way children watch a video or DVD repeatedly and exclusively for days or weeks as Jamie did, and want the same book read again and again.

Repetition and ritual were apparent too in Jamie's engagement with computer games. These involved quite sophisticated manoeuvres as he made predictions, hypothesised and interpreted different symbolic systems, while engaged in interpreting both visual images and print and using sound and movement to make meaning. Returning repeatedly to his favourite screen based interactive games supported his familiarity with content and narrative structure but it also strengthened his understanding of how to make meaning by integrating information from various different formats and across different modes of representation.

It is likely that Jamie's understanding of and familiarity with narrative was developing from his experience of hearing family stories, sharing books and comics, but most of all through TV, film and computer games (Marsh and Millard, 2000). As Jamie watched and re-enacted scenes from his favourite videos at home, he was learning about the structure and conventional features of narrative. He could use this information to inform his own storying as he borrowed from his store of knowledge and created new meanings through play.

### Jamie at nursery

Like the other children, Jamie's involvement with his home world was of prime importance and a constant reference point.

Jamie talks about his collection of videos:

C:  You've got lots of videos as well haven't you?

J:  Yeh. Bob the Builder, Buzz Lightyear ...that's all Michael ever watches ... Buzz

C:  Michael's your brother?

J:  Yeh. That's all he ever watches ...Buzz.

C:  What's your favourite one?

J:  Thank God

C:  Which one do you like best?

J:  Eh. Tots TV

C:  You told me you watched Bob the Builder last night didn't you?

J:  Yeh. I still watch and. and I say (*turns, putting hands on hips*) No I'm not watching Buzz every day (*laughs*) ... I think to meself ... I think to meself Watch a different film or somefing ... Watch, watch Bob or somefing ... or Tweenies.

This short conversation clearly illustrates Jamie's knowledge and interest in film and the social nature of his experiences. His lexical choices, fluctuations in pitch and tone, use of gesture and other non-verbal indicators also reveal his skill in drawing on the oral tradition of his speech community to tell his story with such clarity and humour.

Jamie's conversation also reveals his deep knowledge and familiarity with children's TV and film. Characters from popular culture who were so impor-tant in his everyday experiences at home were also the subject of his talk, occasional drawing and model making at nursery. Jamie's interests were revealed across a wide range of modes of representation and particularly in his play. Either on his own or with other children he was engaged in creating his own plots, and improvising new meanings for his characters, often assuming an authority through role play that was not apparent at other times.

Robinson (1997) suggests a commonality between print and televisual narra-tives, which allows children to learn about the genre and contributes more significantly to their understanding of literacy than learning to read print and images away from the screen. Jamie has a wealth of material in his cultural repertoire on which to draw in his play and in the creation of imaginary worlds.

Jamie, Georgie, Haroun and Katie are outside in the nursery play area, running between two wooden playhouses. They are rolling on the ground:

J.  He's eating us he is (*runs to house 1*). Gate's open, gate's closed (*Haroun presses an imaginary button*)

J.  Can't hear it can we. Go on then. Put your seat belt on

    You've got to weigh yourself

H.  You're bigger

J.  Your turn to weigh Katie. Weigh yourself. (*J. sits on a shelf*)

    A rocket. Hurry up to the space rocket.

    Hurry in the space rocket.

H.  Open it up. (*presses 'button'*) Yah-yah- yah

J.  You can get dead Katie

K.  No, I'm in the space rocket. (*runs back to house 2*)

J.  It's going to go dead isn't it? Quick close the gate. He can't get in now. Don't go out there will you, a monster will get yer.

    (*Katie goes out and lies on the floor. Jamie approaches her*).

J.  Alright? (*She gets up and they run back to house 1*)

    Come on Haroun, it's a shark

H   Shark

J.  It's a space rocket

K.  I want to get out

J.  Shark, Shark

H.  Shark

J.  We're better off in this one. (*moves to house 2*)

In this sequence, the children have entered the realms of fantasy to pursue a theme of good and evil, with a focus on escaping from danger, about which they all implicitly concur. They are key players in situations that draw on several of Jamie's favourite videos with swift action that is linked to computer games. Jamie is a prime mover and has an authority and command that is not manifested in out of play situations, where he tends to be more solitary. He also shows his knowledge of the world of space where astronauts wear seat belts and are weighed before they go onboard. Jamie has been able to show his 'funds of knowledge', including his oral fluency and awareness of appropriate vocabulary in a way that was not apparent at other times. In general, Jamie sought adults rather than children to share his wealth of knowledge about the characters, films and more technical aspects of space travel. Through self initiated play with other children he had become engaged in creating a story from familiar material that demonstrated how he was organising and making sense of his knowledge and experience.

At group storytime Jamie joined in with songs and accompanying hand actions and studied the illustrations in books, but he did not participate in the dialogue and joint sense-making that was encouraged, nor did he volunteer any comment or information as most of the other children did. Although his interests and preoccupations were not marginalised in the nursery, Jamie had already internalised a discourse that endorsed a book based literacy culture.

In the nursery, another child brings a book for Jamie and me to look at:

J:   I don't know how to read. I can't read.

C:   Could you tell me about the story using the pictures?

J:   No, can't read...I can't do nuffink (laughs)

C:   Of course you can

J:   Can't do nuffink (laughs)

## Links between home and school : the third space

The nursery team recognised the importance of giving children opportunities to incorporate their experiences of different media from home. Nick, the nursery teacher, made a film of a train journey from London to Weymouth, he edited it and added a musical soundtrack. The film was on a continuous loop and chairs were set up in front of the TV like seats on a train. Jamie, wearing the train driver's hat provided, sat alone in the 'cabin' staring intently at the screen, which showed the train journey along the south coast. He sang along to the soundtrack, turned to Yasmin who had come to sit in one of the seats and said *I never been to the seaside.* Later he told her *my nanny can't do Play-Station.* He watched the film three times then moved to the nearby 'ticket office' to make some tickets. Jamie's interest was in the visual and aural narratives of home but he showed that he was able to cross boundaries by demonstrating a new understanding of paper based aspects of literacy as part of his play. Jamie's entry to reading and writing was likely to be through his absorbing interest in technology, which was perhaps less visible in a busy nursery than his apparent nonchalant attitude towards the less interactive medium of books.

Jamie had come with a set of expectations about texts, and rules for participating in literacy events which had arisen from his active experiences at home which were in turn shaped by the experiences and assumptions of the two women who cared for him. In the nursery he did not always have opportunities for extended talk and an attentive audience, but through careful observation of his and other children's interests, the staff had planned an environment where Jamie could draw on his cultural resources from home to link with new opportunities for symbolic representation through mark making at school. Through play, supported by the nursery staff, he had created a 'third space' where his narrative skills could develop and he could continue to make meaning through different modes of representation, drawing on his favourite characters from popular culture.

Like the other children, Jamie's literacy learning was a complex activity taking part at the heart of his lived experience. He drew on familiar cultural resources for his own entertainment and self-expression. He was 'stitching together' an identity (Luke and Kale 1997) that incorporated knowledge of oral traditions from his mother and grandparents with scenes and characters from popular culture and putting them to use in new context of the nursery.

* a version of this chapter was published in Gregory, E, Long, S and Volk, D. (eds) (2004) *Many Paths to Literacy,* London: Routledge.

# 7

## Nicole: negotiating a familiar role in an unfamiliar context

*Nicole enters the nursery holding her mother's hand. They have already said goodbye to her sister, whom she often watches through the fence at playtime. Nicole makes quickly for Linda, the nursery nurse who greets her warmly. She happily says good bye to her mum and follows Linda around until she finally settles into playing in the water tray alongside the other children with Linda looking on.*

Nicole's mother Donna was born close to the nursery; the first generation of her family to be educated in the UK since her parents came from Antigua. She visited there for the first time when she was 21 and would like to be able to go back to show her children. Donna attended school locally, leaving at sixteen with qualifications in four subjects. Her eldest sister, who is twenty five years older, helped her with homework; today she helps with babysitting. When Donna left school she worked in a bank in the City of London, sorting cheques and entering them on the computer, as her four sisters had done before her.

Donna talks about the importance of a loving stable environment for her and the children:

> When I was growing up I knew where my home was. I had stability. I knew I was never afraid. I didn't feel lost and I knew where I was going. My dad was there and I've always been there for my kids.

As a teenager, Donna enjoyed taking part in a whole range of sports, particularly gymnastics and although she was no longer actively involved, it was a passion she had passed on to her children David (16), Paul (14), Simone (8) and Nicole. They enjoyed looking at their mother's certificates and badges and she provided a strong model for them as well as acting as occasional coach.

## Nicole's literacy experiences

Nicole loved to do dance and gymnastics and was advanced for her age. She had been recruited by the manager of the local team, despite being officially too young. Donna found her a book on gymnastics at the local charity book-shop and Nicole was very involved in following the moves.

> Nicole loves it. She loves it. She's trying to do the movements in it, the stretches and exercises. The exercises says to stand up, put your arms up like this or with your knees bent or stand up straight. The book shows you the arrows up and down and she knows it's up and down.

Nicole chooses to spend time concentrating on the book. She puts it on the floor and studies it as she moves, following the diagrams in a book written for adults, to help her get it right. What drove her to take meaning from the book was wanting to perfect her moves.

Nicole and her sister Simone had a basket of books at home, traditional tales like *Hansel and Gretel, Cinderella* and *Sleeping Beauty* mostly bought by their mother from the charity shop. The girls brought books home from school. *Where's my Teddy?* was a current favourite which Donna read to them re-peatedly with the result that Nicole *gets the book, sits herself down on the settee, opens it up and reads*. Nicole has memorised the text and can retell the story, using the pictures to help her know when to turn the pages.

Sharing books was a happy and intimate time. The girls cuddled up close to their mother:

> Sometimes I think I'm reading for myself because I do like reading and I don't get time to read and I do try and give it some interest, the way it sounds and then stop and ask them well, why did this happen?

Nicole and Simone sometimes stopped to ask about the pictures or point out something they had spotted. Donna's description of reading at home with Nicole and her sister reveals the peace and pleasure of the activity:

> I think I enjoy it as much as they do. It's unwinding for me as well and it's nice to sit with them. It really does unwind all three of us. And it's peaceful and I can switch off from all the other worries.

The closeness of the experience and the comfort and satisfaction that came from it for mother and daughters is obvious. Donna emphasised the personal benefits of sharing books with the children. Relaxing and switching off from worries enhanced the enjoyment of the activity for all the participants. Sharing a book was conceptualised by Donna as part of her maternal role, providing the best for her children.

The girls spent most of their time together drawing, writing, colouring and sticking, often while lying on the floor in front of a video or children's TV. Sometimes Donna found it hard to stop them when it was time to go to school. She explained how Nicole had *a pink pen and a blue furry telephone book which was her sister's and has the letters of the alphabet in it.* When she has finished writing and drawing she had a ritual of putting the pink pen in the furry book.

The girls also shared books. Simone would read and Nicole would stop her and ask if she could read familiar passages. They played schools with Simone as the teacher, showing her how to do spelling and numbers. Donna says:

> I can hear the chalk writing on the board coming through to my bedroom in the mornings. I can hear them banging away, writing and I can hear Simone saying 'A' 'A'.

> She tells Nicole to copy, like 'and'. She's got to get David's name right, and she does Maths numbers with her.

A diary entry showed that Simone had given her sister a tick and a smiley face for writing her numbers correctly and Nicole shouted for her mum to come and admire her efforts.

Reading, drawing, writing and cutting out were experienced as a female pursuits in both the immediate and extended family. There is enjoyment and solidarity to be had in these activities. Donna relates how Nicole, her sister and her cousins meet up every week-end:

> Well we go to the picture club at East Stratford on a Saturday morning. They can watch a film. They do a bit of colouring before it starts and then they go to their nan's. They play schools and they do writing again, lots of names, make a list of who's in the class. The two older girls are the teachers.

Donna thought it was important that before she went to primary school, Nicole could write all the family names and her address. She was teaching her to find her way home from the local market too.

Literacy also has a functional purpose in the household. Donna liked to *keep up with the news* by reading the newspaper her eldest son brought home. She also made shopping lists which Nicole joined in with. Her independent use of the gymnastics book to teach herself moves, suggests that Nicole had internalised this view. Literacy was embedded in other activities associated with family life so Nicole was learning about it on many different levels.

## Nicole at nursery

At school Nicole was quiet, passive and reticent and often to be found watching other children's activities from the sidelines. She did not volunteer information unless persuaded and was not fully engaged, rarely taking initiative. She followed instructions from other children or members of staff, silently tapping the adults whenever she wanted attention.

At storytime she enthusiastically took part in the songs and actions and listened to the story with a look of serious concentration, often joining in with repeated refrains from the text, but she did not respond to the adult's questions unless she was specifically asked. On one occasion, following a request from the nursery teacher, she went to the front of the group and confidently pointed out the place on the page at which the reading should start.

She enjoyed sharing a picture book with an adult and would competently turn the pages, point to and label items in the pictures but she did not talk about events in the story. If another child was involved she was more cautious in her responses and would listen rather than actively participate. In one to one interactions with adults she could retell familiar stories such as the *Three Billy Goats Gruff* in sequence, using story language and with obvious enjoyment. She signalled her interest in TV and film at home by bringing a *Tweenies* video to nursery. She sat holding the cover and watching the screen silently alongside five other children who were chatting boisterously and joining in with the actions.

It was hard to equate Nicole's behaviour in the nursery with the child who confidently consulted an adult book on gymnastics to practise her exercises. On occasions however, Nicole's hidden resources were revealed. Singing appeared to offer her a safe place from which to project herself and literally and metaphorically find her voice. At these times she would be transformed, participating enthusiastically in songs sung by children and adults. A nursery nurse had told Nicole's mother that she *sings louder than she talks*.

Nicole's interactions with children and adults in the nursery appeared to reflect her role at home, where as the youngest child and little sister she was not required to be autonomous or make decisions. Home based literacy activities were collaborative but mostly initiated by her older sisters and cousins. The drawing, writing, reading and storying that took place in a range of familiar

**Figure 7.1 Nicole's picture**

local contexts created and sustained a bond with female members of her family.

Nicole's reticence may have been related to her unfamiliarity with the goals of the nursery, which were to foster independence and autonomy through self initiated activity. Her route to literacy at home was through a solidarity that was not readily available outside that familiar context. Peer relationships and social bonding were key features in the learner identities of many of the children who were proactive in interacting with others and in pursuing their own interests and concerns. Nicole's silence may have been due to confusion about her role at nursery, which conflicted with her identity as the youngest sibling.

Occasionally Nicole spontaneously engaged in mark-making at nursery, which incorporated her practices from home:

Nicole is writing family names, covering the paper with numbers and letter-like shapes

N:  I'm drawing mummy's window

C.  What can she see out of her window?

N:  The moon... and a pig. That's the door and her eyes.

Now she's opening the door.

She picks up the scissors and proficiently cuts her picture into four uneven pieces. She takes some masking tape and sticks one very small piece of paper to the largest.

Nicole is demonstrating her sense of intention. Kress (1997) and Pahl (1999) have both suggested that the child's purpose in cutting out their pictures is to move their work from the page into the physical environment to make objects three dimensional and real. Most of the capabilities that Nicole shows in this episode were not generally visible in the nursery but hidden behind her passive and reticent exterior. The numbers and letters and other symbols were perhaps a reminder of playing school with her sister.

## Linking home and school: the third space

Nicole's possible route into literacy learning took everyone by surprise. It manifested itself after she had been in the nursery for almost a year. Twins aged three and a half came to visit the nursery while their mother discussed arrangements for them to join the class in September. Nicole took charge almost immediately, leading them by the hand to a range of activities and in doing so collected a number of other girls. At the top of her voice she initiated songs such as *A Sailor Went to Sea* and *Ring a Ring a Roses*, to which only she knew the second verse. She stopped everyone to correct their singing mistakes or to teach the correct actions. She told children when to be quiet because 'the babies' might be frightened. She took them outside to the climbing frame where she showed the agility and flexibility her mother had proudly spoken of, and then led them to the graphics area where she gave them pens and paper and launched into mark making herself, making a 'letter' composed of pieces of paper covered with drawing and some scattered letter-like shapes, bound with masking tape.

On joining the nursery Nicole had encountered familiar texts and tools for literacy learning. She encountered story reading, recognised songs, action rhymes and opportunities for joining in dance, despite often being too shy to do so. Her regular drawing, writing and cutting out sessions with her sister and cousins had familiarised her with play based learning and given her a sense of what she could expect when she went to school. But the contradictions she encountered between home and school appeared to relate to her role as an autonomous learner away from the close and loving contact with familiar adults and children and the expectations of children's independence and agency which were implicit in the nursery's philosophy.

The nursery presented all the children with new literacy experiences but for some this was more of a challenge. Studies like those of Shirley Brice Heath (see chapter 2) have shown how children whose interactions with literacy in their homes and communities match those of school can make a smoother transition that can ultimately enhance their success as literacy learners. Nicole's experience is a reminder that this is not just in terms of practices; she was used to sharing and talking about books and words, and could do so confidently in one to one situations, although she generally chose not to do so at school. It was in the roles and relationships that surrounded these events that Nicole appeared to be uncomfortable. Book sharing was not enough in itself to give her continuity of experience.

The striking change in Nicole's behaviour when the young twins arrived suggested that she understood the role she should play as an older more experienced member of the nursery community. It seemed that she could identify with these younger children. This was the third space, where the worlds of home and school met and Nicole felt able to display the funds of knowledge that had previously not been apparent to the nursery staff. The surprising change in her demeanour and attitude revealed her confidence and assertiveness in a context where she understood what was expected of her.

# 8

## Asif: literacy and learning
## a new language

*Asif runs into the nursery, his father close behind him. They exchange goodbyes in Bengali and Asif moves to the computer, where two boys are using the mouse to select nursery rhymes. Asif points to something on the screen and smiles when one of the boys turns to him in response. As they leave to play outside, Asif takes over, experimenting with moving the cursor.*

Asif's father and mother came to the UK from Bangladesh two years ago when he was a year old. They were living in London while his father, Anwar, who had worked as a lawyer in Dhaka, was completing a Law degree at the University of London. Asif's mother, who had an MA in public administration from the University of Dhaka, was working in a local superstore because she did not feel confident about her spoken English.

### Asif's literacy experiences

In Dhaka, Anwar had *a big secretarial table* which was piled with papers, books and leaflets connected with his work, all of which was conducted in English. Asif would see his father reading newspapers and his mother reading women's magazines in Bengali. His father would recite rhymes in Bengali that he remembered from his childhood and rhymes in English such as *Mary had a little lamb*.

In Dhaka, Asif lived with his extended family, which included older cousins who attended an English medium school. The children had access to their own television so could make choices about which of the 64 satellite channels they watched, often choosing cartoons in English. They also spoke to each other in English and it is likely they were aware, from the experience of their father, uncles and grandfather, that it was a prestigious language connected to professional success.

In England Asif saw his father studying and often sat with him when he was reading, sometimes bringing his own books and a request to read them. Anwar often stopped to take time to share books in Bengali brought from Bangladesh and in English from the nursery. He would read the book and then tell Asif what it was about.

Both parents helped Asif write the letters of the English alphabet, often drawing dots for him to join, because *he will need that in school.* Although they wanted him to be literate in Bengali and know Arabic so he could take part in religious duties, they were concentrating on literacy in English first because *We think at the moment it's better for him to learn one language and it's English because he's facing it every day.*

In many ways, Asif was learning in the same way his father did. Anwar remembers his own early education at school in Bangladesh:

> They teach you how to write, letters, then word-making then sentences. How to pronounce and how to write. We had children's books, alphabet books and rhymes.

His parents encouraged Asif to speak both English and Bengali and they took the lead from him:

> We speak to him in Bangla and he replies in Bangla. Nowadays he wants to speak English at home. When he speaks in English I reply in English.

Asif was also learning English from the TV, particularly *The Teletubbies* and *Tweenies.*

> He's just crazy about them. He starts jumping and singing with them and he repeats what they say.

It is clear that Asif was growing up in a rich language environment, surrounded by people who spoke both Bengali and English. He watched and listened to his mother praying each day in Arabic and copied her actions. He saw written language used for pleasure and leisure but he was no doubt aware that literacy was also connected to the religious and professional worlds.

The family chose the nursery because there were *less Sylheti speaking children than in others in the area and more English people.* Sajjad explains that he finds Sylheti (a dialect of Bengali) difficult to understand because of the different vocabulary. He is very clear that he only wants Asif to speak Bengali. Within his family tradition, language choices are directly linked to professional and social life and to class affiliations.

Asif's father's fluency in English meant that he had more involvement with his son's literacy learning and these were special times between them. He provided a model for Asif to identify with and it is likely that he was already making the connection that choice of language is an important issue for his family, connected with status and employment. Anwar explains:

> World wide English is so demanded. If you don't speak English you can't apply for a better job. You face, what can I say, difficulties to find anything better.

To be literate in Bengali and English is a high priority and linked to ways of succeeding in the world. When I asked Anwar what he hoped for his son when he grew up, he replied that Asif would choose what he wanted to be but that whatever it was, *he will go to the peak, the apex of that particular profession.*

## Asif at nursery

In the nursery Asif enjoyed social encounters with other children but his emerging English and initial unfamiliarity with Sylheti made it difficult for him to communicate. He especially wanted to be part of a group of older boys whose abiding interest was the computer. Asif was often to be found standing at the edge of their games, observing them, copying their actions by writing his name on the list to indicate that he wanted to use the computer. But he was constrained by the 'double bind', as identified by Tabors (1997:35):

> In any language learning situation in natural circumstances, communicative competence and social competence are inextricably linked; the double bind is that each is necessary for the development of the other.

Because Asif's emergent English prevented him from fully engaging in the social activities of the group, the boys did not initiate interactions with him and on the occasions that he did try to join in with their play, they seldom responded to him.

Asif spent long periods engaged in solitary activities, sometimes watching other children, sometimes in a mode which Suzi Long (2002) describes as 'tuned out', gazing out of the window, blinking repeatedly or staring at objects unrelated to the task in hand. He found that learning a new language and a new culture was an exhausting and demanding business. Having time out to listen to a tape in his first language provided security, familiarity and the opportunity to switch off for a while.

From term 1 he actively sought out the company and involvement of other children.

> Asif gets a book and sits on the carpet between two children
> He holds up his thumb to one who doesn't look up but says
> 'Yes'.

> Asif is looking at *Where's Spot.* He lifts the flap and
> shows the picture underneath to Fameeda. She helps him
> to turn the next page.

Songs and rhymes were important to Asif. At group story time, he preferred to join in with either the singing or doing the actions – although he found it difficult to do both at the same time – rather than listening to a story which he did not always understand. One day while he was at the playdough table, listening to a visitor to the nursery who was playing his guitar, he told me: *My family sing Baa baa black sheep and Ring a ring a garden.*

As he became more proficient in English, often as a result of his own agency, Asif became more socially integrated, although not yet with the older boys he aspired to play with.

In term 2 Stacey, a British monolingual child, and Asif were in the dramatic play area involved in domestic role play. Asif was lying on the bed while Stacey was at the stove.

> S   I do breakfast now
>
> A   I do baby
>
> Asif stands up and they start banging yogurt pots together
>
> S   Them my baby (holding a doll)
>
> A   Them my baby (getting one too)
>
> They try to put on animal slippers, one each
>
> A   I open my shoes
>
> S   Stick it in you silly billy (his foot)
>
> A   I want my one now
>
> S   And mine
>
> A   And mine
>
> S   And mine
>
> They laugh, put their shoes on and walk off with their dolls.

Role play opportunities such as this enabled Asif to take more risks with his language learning than he did when sharing a book. Here he was rehearsing and echoing Stacey's words as well as experimenting with chunks of language ( I do baby/ I want my one now), using what he knows creatively ( I open my shoes). Asif has created his own zone of proximal development. The dramatic play, obviously a source of enjoyment to both children, has freed him from other constraints and shows how he elicits the support of other children to help him learn the new language. The story that is beginning to emerge from their play as they walk off with their 'babies' is also informing their under-standing of narrative.

### Books and stories

Asif employed a range of unconscious strategies through playful encounters to make and take meaning from texts in a new language. In the following example, he and Margaret, a nursery nurse, are looking at *Where's My Kitten?* Another child, who has been listening to *Peace At Last* in Bengali, unplugs the headphones while the tape is still running and the story can be heard loudly in the background:

A:  That good Bangla.

　　 See the book now.

　　 What that one?

　　 Quack

M:  Yes, it's a duck. A yellow duck

A:  Who that there? (pointing to a snake)

　　 Look

　　 I don't like it

M:  Have you seen a snake?

A:  Look

M:  Yes, two snakes. When did you see a snake Asif?

A   I don't like it (pointing to a monkey)

M   Why don't you like the monkey?

A:  I like it (pointing to a frog)

M:  Do you like the frog?

A    Yes.

M:   What's that one? The red...?

A    Dog. I like it.

     Let see outside (turns back to look at the book cover)

———————

M:   What's there Asif?

A:   There two

M:   Two what?

A    One cat, butterfly, cat.

M:   What's the cat doing?

A:   I like owl, I got owl. My owl talking.

M:   Does it talk? Where does your owl live?

A:   Home

M:   What does it say when it talks

A:   Water.

     I go with my friend. Bye.

This interaction around a book exemplifies many of the learning opportunities that Asif involved himself in during his day to day activities in the nursery. His expression of surprise and pleasure: *That good Bangla* is a recognition of his daily experience of moving between languages and an acknowledgement of his first language which, although familiar to many children when read aloud, was not spoken by them in the nursery. The extract also demonstrates Asif's current understanding of reading and book sharing. He uses the interaction as a means of learning and rehearsing English. He ignores, or does not understand, the questions and pursues his own strategies, applying formulaic responses: *I like it* or *I don't like it,* to the pictures which he understands to carry meaning. He is also using the pictures as visual aids to practice labelling, in particular the names of animals, 'dog' 'cat' 'butterfly'. However, when he feels confident he goes beyond labelling or counting to volunteer information about his toy owl. His agency in this encounter, which he initiates and concludes, is obvious. It is his agenda they are working to and he is drawing on previous experiences of book sharing to take control by asking questions, using imperatives, and making suggestions.

His pleasure in rehearsing and repeating words and enjoying their sounds was obvious at other times when he engaged with print:

> Asif is looking at *Brown Bear, Brown Bear What Do You See*
> while waiting for group story to begin. He repeats 'black,
> black, black' and laughs.

> Asif is sitting in the book area on his own looking at *The Very Hungry
> Caterpillar.* In a sing song voice, he repeats, 'one apple, one apple,
> one apple' and then speaks to himself in Bengali.

> Asif is sitting at the computer alone. He says 'look' to some children
> standing nearby, points to the screen and says 'why oh why oh why'.

While adding to his store of known words, Asif is enjoying the timbre of English and building his confidence. However, he also takes advantage of interacting with another child to jointly construct meaning.

> Michelle and Asif are sitting in the book area sharing *The Doorbell Rang*
>
> Michelle has a pointer which she is running under the words.
>
> M:  The Doorbell
>
> A:  Rang
>
>     1,2,3,4,5 (pointing to the biscuits on the plate)
>
> M   That's his cousins (pointing to the children in the picture)
>
> A   I like this story.

## Links between home and school: third space

In the nursery Asif encountered books, stories, songs and rhymes; genres that he was familiar with from home in both English and Bengali. But there were incongruencies and contradictions in his experiences too. He did not see the letters of the alphabet being explicitly taught as he did at home and he rarely chose to draw or mark make. At home the main language of communication was Bengali or English whereas in the nursery, while the staff spoke English, many of the children spoke to each other in Sylheti so Asif had to become familiar with it.

His interest and preoccupation appeared to be in the familiar activities of labelling and counting, rather then the shared story reading which, as we have seen, was central to the pedagogical practices of literacy learning in the nursery. He also adopted a proactive approach to communicating with other children and playing alongside them. His third space, for the time being at least, appeared to be at a linguistic level which enabled him to combine his knowledge and experience of story and play from home with the demands of learning English. The informality of the nursery environment and philosophy of independence and self initiated play based activities supported him in doing this.

Asif was learning the new culture of the nursery through the medium of a new language. We can see that this was a huge undertaking for a young child because of the social, emotional and cognitive demands it made on him away from the security of his family. His entry into literacy in English initially seemed to be mainly as a vehicle for learning a language which was so prized by his extended family and which he needed so he could communicate with his peers.

# 9

## What the children tell us: Policy implications and practical strategies

**This concluding chapter is in two parts. Part One summarises the individual literacy patterns of each of the children observed in this study and discusses the issues they experience, the implications for their literacy development and for nursery practice.**

**Part Two uses the findings of the study to suggest a framework for understanding and responding appropriately to young children's individual literate identities. The book ends with practical strategies for developing literacy in the early years.**

This glimpse of the six children's experiences at home and in the nursery tells about the ways in which they were learning literacy through activities that had meaning for them. The children were living in different social and cultural contexts that gave rise to significant variation in how they related to literacy when they came to nursery. Although there were commonalities, what stood out was the individuality of each child's experience.

**Kabir** spoke Sylheti-Bengali and was learning about literacy in Bengali, English and Arabic: three different languages and scripts, each with a distinctive set of expectations and practices. As he became more familiar with the medium of English, he appeared to be able to move between languages, easing himself into the literacy world of the nursery in English, tapping into his knowledge of Bengali through audiotapes, books and signs but reserving his evolving knowledge of Arabic for his home life.

**Michelle** was experiencing the pleasure and satisfaction that can accompany both formal and informal learning as she practised writing accurately with her mother, talking about books brought from the library, and singing and dancing in front of the television with her sister. She was actively engaged in recreating those contexts in her play in the nursery. For her there appeared to be a continuity between the practises of home and school, even though there was little formal teaching in the nursery.

**Sadia** spoke Sylheti-Bengali and was learning to be literate in three other languages Bengali, Arabic and English. She experienced literacy as a serious endeavour which the whole family engaged in together and she also learned about school literacy from role play with her sisters. The cultural model of literacy learning that was rooted in Sadia's family was not one that was shared by the nursery, where pedagogy was shaped by the recognised principles concerning young children's learning and development. Play was the dominant paradigm for learning; copying and recitation were not valued as learning strategies. Sadia was intelligent and learned quickly but she was confused and unsettled in the nursery. She appeared not to recognise the rules for participation and seemed not to know what was expected of her.

**Jamie** was developing an understanding of literacy learning through multi-modal texts and audiovisual narratives that were more closely aligned to his family's oral culture. Jamie's experience of literacy at home was strongly related to his interest in popular culture. Jamie and his brother repeatedly inhabited different characters and role played familiar scenes from films, supported and encouraged by their mother and grandmother who bought them videos and computer games. His familiarity with computer games gave him a confidence in non print based literacy practices. He drew selectively on this wealth of knowledge to pursue his interests in the nursery.

**Nicole** seemed to be engaged in literacy for an immediate purpose which was connected to her role as the youngest child in a close family and the contentment that came from play and collaboration with female relatives. The precision and manual dexterity she had developed as a result of her frequent engagement with paper based activities were evident in her mark making. Her fluency, confidence and familiarity with books and stories emerged in one to one interactions with an adult, but in the nursery she did not initiate any of the activities with which she was so familiar at home. She was usually silent and withdrawn at nursery, playing alone or watching from the sidelines.

**Asif** was an emergent bilingual, the first child in his family to receive formal education in the UK. He was part of a network of relatives in Bangladesh who spoke Bengali but were educated through the medium of English which they used for academic and professional purposes and which the younger members used as the main medium of communication. Asif was at an early stage of learning English and at nursery he chose familiar stories, rhymes and computer games as resources for his play, actively looking for support from peers to help him make meaning. By doing so he was developing his fluency in English.

These literacy portraits of the children reveal their cultural and linguistic resources, the individuality of their identities as literacy learners and the choices each child made about how to relate to the meanings and practices that were available to them in the nursery.

## Children creating the third space

The children's agency was obvious in creating a third space where their 'funds of knowledge' from home became visible – a meeting place for the worlds of home and school. For Kabir it was in exchanges with other boys that enabled him to draw on his bi-cultural experience. For Michelle it was through her collaborative activities with a group of other girls when gender roles could be discussed and rehearsed and represented by talk, songs, dance and on paper. For Sadia it was in finding activities that had rules and tangible outcomes. For Jamie it was in his preoccupation and involvement with characters from popular culture, his knowledge of media texts and multiple modes of representation. For Nicole, it was in finding a situation where she understood what was expected of her and for Asif it was to draw on his knowledge of meaning making in Bengali for rehearsing English through the medium of picture books and dramatic play.

The children demonstrated sophistication in the varied ways each introduced and combined elements of their experience and most demonstrated agency and intention in drawing on their current understandings of literacy as well as developing new ones. They created their own zones of proximal development and used their own funds of knowledge to solve problems. Kabir drew on the familiar strategy of watching, listening and repeating as a learning strategy when he first joined the nursery. Michelle's preoccupation with accurate spelling of family names at home gave her an interest in talking about transcriptional elements of writing in school. Jamie extended his interest in video and popular culture from home to explore mark making in the nursery.

The children were actively engaged in pursuing their own interests. In their first year in the nursery, they were busy making links with the familiar world of home through participating in activities that were repeated as familiar rituals.

Most did so with the support of other children or adults. Literacy was integral to these activities rather than being the children's purpose or sole outcome.

## The individuality of children's relationships with literacy

Each child's relationship with literacy pointed to both connections and difference in the practices, materials, the languages of literacy and tacit theories that operated beneath the surface. For Sadia and Kabir it was a connection with heritage and extended family networks separated by distance; for Nicole, Kabir and Jamie it was connected to bonding with siblings. Literacy learning in its various guises appeared to be a source of pleasure and satisfaction for all the children

We saw how through interactions with important people in their lives, the children learned how literacy was understood, valued and practised within their families. But it was also upheld and promoted within the wider community. Kabir's sisters went to Mosque school to learn Bengali and Arabic, Michelle and her mother borrowed books from the library, Sadia and Nicole had books and Jamie video and computer games bought for them from the local shops.

The children were also becoming aware that literacy had associations that went beyond their immediate community context. Literacy in Asif's family had a professional association through the practice of Law. Literacy gave the families of Sadia, Asif and Kabir access to guidance for how to lead an honourable life as a Muslim. For Michelle's mother there were connections with school success, self esteem and employment. Each child's developing orientation to and understanding of literacy in their family was based on specific familial circumstances and experiences, set within broader cultural and community traditions and institutional practices.

Such snapshots of experience show that, as the New Literacy Studies discussed in Chapter 2 suggests, literacy changes according to context and purpose and the process has links to wider influences outside the home. There were differences that made the children's understanding of literacy distinct and unique, but the children also shared similarities and connections across their experiences.

## Similarities in the children's home experiences

Each family possessed its own cultural models of literacy yet there were some commonalities in the children's lives. All the children:

- had significant and influential interactions around literacy with siblings and members of their extended family

- experienced forms of literacy learning that were mediated by talk of various kinds

- had informal experiences of literacy where the goal was understanding the message contained in the print

- had experience of literacy where the medium was instruction, sometimes through play

- had experience of popular culture and media texts

- were taught the alphabet in English or Bengali script or both.

## Differences in the children's home experience

The children's stories show how they entered the nursery already positioned in relation to literacy through their family history and traditions and their social interactions with important people in their lives. Conversations with parents revealed both their concern to uphold cultural affiliations that connected generations and the deep personal connections between their own experiences of literacy learning and those they engaged in with their children. Also apparent were the modifications and adaptations they had incorporated to account for new practices, texts and technologies. For example, Kabir's mother combined knowledge from her experience as a teaching assistant with her own childhood experience of learning through recitation and copying. Jamie's grandmother taught him the alphabet, as she had her daughters, but she also bought him multimedia programmes for the computer. Michelle's mother taught her how to spell family names but also recorded educational programmes from satellite television so that Michelle could revisit them. Figure 9.1 (page 82) shows how each child's experience was distinctive because it was influenced by unique configurations of various factors.

### Challenging assumptions

Considerations of children's success in school are often concerned with locating them as members of a group based on, for example, economic status, ethnicity or language. These overarching categories appear more obvious than more subtle cultural variations. The children's stories challenge the generalisations that often fail to take into account the individual nature of children's understanding of literacy. For example, Kabir, Sadia and Asif were all bilingual and of Bangladeshi heritage but their identities as literacy learners and ex-

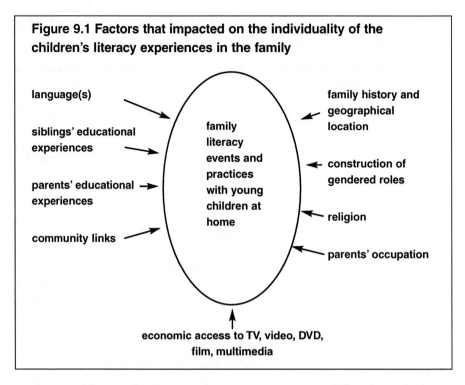

**Figure 9.1 Factors that impacted on the individuality of the children's literacy experiences in the family**

language(s)

siblings' educational experiences

parents' educational experiences

community links

family literacy events and practices with young children at home

family history and geographical location

construction of gendered roles

religion

parents' occupation

economic access to TV, video, DVD, film, multimedia

periences of literacy learning in the nursery were very different. Such divergence went beyond learning styles to much deeper differences in each child's world in relation to family history and practices, languages and expectations of what constituted school literacy learning.

### Finding their feet in the nursery

As the children stepped into the world of the nursery, each with their own orientation to literacy learning, they encountered new school literacy experiences and expectations, such as group storytime, book-making, taking the register, signing up to use the computer or finding their name on a place-mat at lunchtime. We saw how each child was negotiating a role for themselves which made connections with their experiences at home. However, there appeared to be key factors or themes that were significant for their engagement with literacy in their first year in the nursery. These were:

- understanding the nursery pedagogy
- the significance of gender
- media and popular culture

### *Understanding the nursery pedagogy*

Unlike families, early years staff have formal knowledge of the curriculum, an understanding of child development acquired in their training, and a specific vocabulary to talk about what makes successful learning. In a community of practice such as an early years setting, this taken for granted knowledge may not be obvious to those outside it. For example Bernstein (1990, 1996) argues that in the invisible pedagogy of an early years classroom children are expected to be 'busy' and 'doing' so that judgements can be made by staff about their stage of development. Practice in the nursery was based on principles about literacy learning based on a child centred philosophy. This meant that children were expected to learn through play, to be active in pursuing their interests and to show autonomy in initiating and sustaining their play with other children and adults. But there were also adult initiated activities, such as group storytime, book-making or recipe writing following a cooking session, where the children's choice and control were restricted and power relations were more apparent.

Although information was open to parents through policy documents or welcome booklets, there was a great deal about learning in the nursery that was left unsaid, particularly the more subtle and less visible elements. As we have seen, some children such as Michelle and Kabir accepted and thrived within the invisible pedagogy, Jamie and Asif adopted it selectively for their own purposes but sometimes appeared confused. Nicole and particularly Sadia appeared not to understand the implicit rules for participation.

The social dimension of literacy learning for most of the children in the nursery was inextricably bound with the pleasure and satisfaction that arose from interaction and joint achievement. The role of mediators, whether adults or children, was an important component in helping most of the children accomplish specific purposes which involved literacy and enabling them to achieve more than they could have on their own. But as the children's stories show, the relationships were not dependent or passive.

Kabir, Michelle, and to a certain extent Asif, who had experienced some deliberate teaching strategies and more formal learning relationships at home, enjoyed familiarity with classroom relations and their self regulation facilitated their literacy learning. Within the rules and expectations implicit in the nursery pedagogy, they were able to pursue their own interests and concerns, enlisting the support of adults or children as necessary. Kabir, in the company of other boys, was learning how to take meaning from books in a way that reflected their bi-cultural experience. Nicole, however, found relationships more problematic because they did not reflect the warmth, closeness and dependency she experienced at home. She was unaccustomed to initiating activities or exchanges and did not appear to understand the expectations for interacting with adult members of staff. Sadia too could not fully access the implicit rules for successful nursery learning. Jamie, whose experience at home was of a predominantly adult culture, was able to pursue his interest in video and film but mainly as a solitary activity. He constantly sought the company of adults and this was disapproved of within the nursery discourse of independence and peer support.

### The significance of gender

Judith Solsken (1995) and David Barton (2007) draw attention to the deep connections between gender and literacy and this relationship was reflected in the dynamics of the children's literacy learning particularly in relation to peer group solidarity. Asif's aspirations to join a dominant group of boys at the computer were no doubt sparked by his recognition of the high status they attributed to this activity. For Michelle (in the nursery) and Nicole (with her sister and female cousins at home) drawing, writing, cutting and sticking were habitual activities that reinforced gender affiliations. At these times, literacy was often used as a focus for trying out adult roles, particularly through the accompanying talk. Talk was important for the boys too. Kabir, following the lead from his peers, was preoccupied with popular artefacts such as motorbikes, monsters and space rockets and used this to rehearse gendered attitudes and behaviours. Jamie's identification was with male popular heroes, Buzz Lightyear and Bob the Builder, about whom he constantly wanted to talk with adults.

Despite the ethos of the nursery which discouraged children from behaving in stereotypical gender oriented ways, gender affiliations were significant for the children. Gendered aspects of literacy learning were not always immediately visible, but were potentially problematic for the staff. There was a tension between encouraging children to follow their own interests and concerns and being aware that gendered activity could channel and constrain children's behaviour.

### Media and popular culture

One of the key ways in which the children made their own links between the worlds of home and school was through media and popular culture. Heroes from popular culture and his home world of film and computer games appeared in Jamie's drawings and model making. An interest in popular music was integral to Michelle's projected life as a teenage girl, which she habitually represented through singing, dancing, talk and mark-making.

For Asif, who was actively enlisting support from adults and children to learn a new language, access to stories on audiotape in his familiar home language was a source of pleasure and solace. Video and filmed nursery activities were a medium for learning English. Kabir and Michelle's fascination with multimedia at school had its origins in their adept use of the TV remote control at home to play interactive games. For Kabir it was also an active way of learning English through the peer group talk that surrounded use of the computer.

Although Sadia's pleasure and interest in the Teletubbies at home was not evident in the nursery, she could sometimes be seen watching recordings of nursery role play and storytelling activities from her chosen vantage point near the maths activities. Nicole's familiarity with TV and film was revealed when she brought a video from home to be played in the nursery and from the songs she sang, which helped her to signal her presence. It seems that even for the quietest children and those who were least comfortable with school literacy learning, media texts were a connection with home.

Most of the children expanded their experiences of TV and video at home to the new worlds of digital technology available in the nursery. Nick, the nursery teacher, explicitly demonstrated and promoted multimodal texts, presenting children with new possibilities for taking and making meaning and crossing boundaries through the combination of sound, image and movement.

Thanks to advancements in technology, digital media such as computer games, interactive TV and mobile phones are increasingly available to children and their families. These technologies have caused significant shifts in children's literacy lives because they demand and created new skills, knowledge and understanding and new ways of communicating. This meant the children saw themselves differently to the way their teachers had done as children. If, as Jackie Marsh ( 2005) has argued and the six children's experiences affirm, popular culture and new media have become a central part of children's 'life worlds', these cannot be left at the nursery door.

## Looking back and looking forward

The children's stories show the complex, shifting dynamic nature of their literate identities. They drew on cultural resources from home which had themselves been redefined over generations, and they observed and engaged in new social practices and technologies as a rehearsal for their own roles as literate adults in a new media age. The children were creatively blending understandings from their involvement with the different worlds of home and school and for some of them this meant knowing that certain aspects of their lives at home were to be kept separate.

The process of looking back and looking forward might help to explain how change was both accommodated and constructed by the children who inhabited different sometimes contradictory cultural worlds. As the children used their knowledge and experiences from home to learn about literacy in the new cultural site of the nursery, they were developing a new understanding of the possibilities of literacy which would facilitate new literate identities and contribute to the multidimensional nature of their literacy experience.

This book has explored children's understanding of literacy and presented a picture of six children at home and at school and the ways in which they created links between their experiences in different contexts. This study does not suggest that the way forward lies in designing a single pedagogy that will fit all learners. It indicates, rather, that diversity should be embraced as strength, that literate identities can sit comfortably with each other and that combinations and configurations can result in new ways of being literate.

## Implications for policy

The stories of these six young children show that each brought with them a unique relationship with literacy when they came to the nursery and each was engaged in making their own links by combining their experiences of the different worlds of home and school. The message for educationalists is clear:

- Firstly, it is important to regard parents as partners, especially when gathering information about children's home literacy experiences
- Secondly, the nursery environment should enable young children to make their own connections while also getting help from practitioners when they need it.

This philosophy is embedded in the *Early Years Foundation Stage Curriculum* (DfES, 2007) through its four main principles that emphasise the uniqueness of each child and the need for staff to develop shared knowledge with parents and adopt flexible inclusive practices that acknowledge and build on the diversity of experience.

## Part Two
## A framework for understanding young children's unique literate identities

Figure 9.2 (page 88) presents a framework I developed as a result of my research. It offers a visual representation of the complexity of literacy learning for young children and an illustration of the largely invisible influences that make each child's experience unique. It interprets literacy learning as a dynamic process in which, as we have seen, young children show creative agency but may be left behind if they are not supported in making connections between their different literate worlds. Implications arise from the model of literacy learning offered by the framework. The next section examines policy and practice that might support this model and makes suggestions for how children who struggled such as Sadia and Nicole, might be helped to find congruencies, the comfortable overlaps that could help them create their own third spaces.

### Helping children find a role as a learner in a new context

The research discussed in this book demonstrates how the six young children navigated their way into literacy learning in the nursery by following their own agendas and preoccupations. They were able to make connections with familiar practices, attitudes, interests, languages, texts or social relationships. Four of them appeared to find their own links and intersections, but Sadia and Nicole appeared to need direct support when tensions and contradictions made the gap too wide for them to bridge. Helping children to develop confidence and feel they belong depends on knowing their previous experience and helping them make connections so that they can capitalise on it in a different context.

For these children, who were at the early stages of learning English, the importance of hearing and using their home language was not just a comfort or a recognition of their home experience. It was a necessary factor to ensure their learning and development would not be restricted by a language that was emerging.

### Listening to parents

In early years settings where opportunities are created to listen regularly to families and children talk about home experiences, interests and achievements, a dialogue can be created where each party has knowledge that will inform the other. This means that the individuality of each child will become

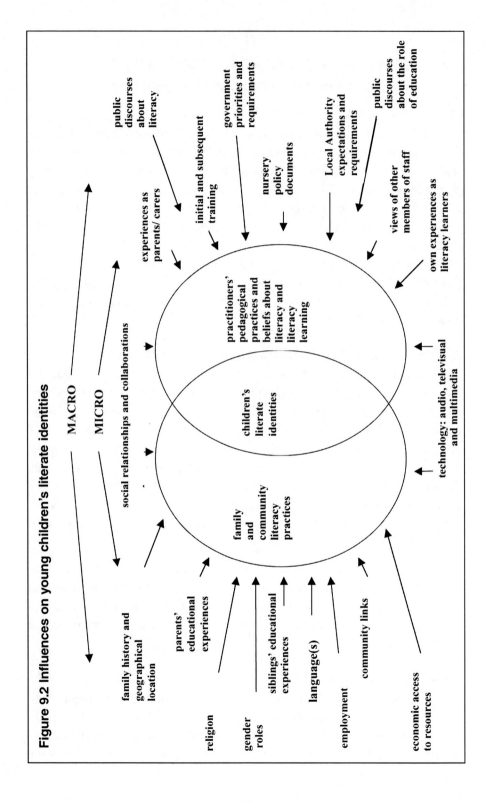

Figure 9.2 Influences on young children's literate identities

more apparent enabling greater insights to be made into their learning. Such opportunities can allow parents to talk about their hopes and expectations in relation to all areas of the child's learning, including language and literacy. It will give members of the nursery team valuable information about the child and also the opportunity to address individual parents' questions and concerns. The role of key workers and practitioners is crucial: strengthening their relationship with the child and the family provides an important point of contact for both. Knowledge about a child's cultural practices and language uses enables practitioners to prepare the nursery environment appropriately for the child. Iram Siraj-Blatchford and Priscilla Clarke (2000 p96) have compiled a list to help those working with young children gain information about children's experience and parents' expectations and beliefs. This could be used in conjunction with the framework referred to above (see figure 9.2) to understand more about the individuality of children's experience of literacy.

Home visits have become common practice in most early years settings. They provide an opportunity for the key practitioner to introduce themselves in a an unhurried way, find out about the child's experiences at home and meet parents and families on their own territory. Home visits also provide a sign for the child that the parent sees the visitor as an important, safe person in the nursery. It might also be an opportunity to take photos for a profile book so the child has a visual reminder of home when they arrive in the nursery. Home visits are part of an important strategy for signalling the desire to make a bridge between home and school but this could have even more meaning and effect if it was followed up by a review six weeks later. The time between enables relationships to develop so a dialogue can be based on the staff's knowledge of the child, and the parents can talk more about the response of their child to the new context of the nursery.

Early Years practitioners are already skilled listeners but it seems important to make explicit to parents that the staff are committed to relating to parents and families on an individual basis and that they see diversity as strength and a benefit for all children. For example, the use of interpreters for meetings signals to families that their voice counts. Other suggestions are discussed later.

### Creating opportunities for children to use their cultural resources

Sadia's involvement in literacy activities at home was not visible in the nursery, where, we have seen, she was an on-looker. Perhaps this would not be the case if copying could be included as a strategy for developing writing. Developmental approaches to mark making and teaching writing encourage young children to draw on knowledge of familiar signs and symbols to represent their message. This approach ensures that the more creative compositional aspects of writing (the message and finding ways to communicate) are not constrained by the transcriptional elements (the secretarial skills of writing). It also enables children to draw on familiar experience from home along with their developing knowledge of the English orthographic system. But since this approach may not be one with which all children are comfortable, practitioners might consider employing other approaches too. For a child like Sadia, for instance, giving direct encouragement to copy from a favourite book, or from labels and signs around the room would acknowledge familiar practices and offer her a starting point with which she felt secure. This might be extended if an adult scribed Sadia's words in her own book, thus showing her new ways of mark making, as promoted in the nursery. Being open and committed to the diversity of children's experience may require the nursery team to consider whether practices based on professional beliefs are meeting the needs of all the children adequately.

### Establishing home school projects where the lead comes from family

Some family literacy programmes are based on an implicit assumption that families do not have the knowledge, skills or experience necessary for their children to become literate. We see this for instance when school related practices such as storybook reading are introduced into family life without an acknowledgement of literacy experiences that are already taking place. A family literacy project which focused on finding out about children's cultural knowledge and experience might be more appropriate. For example family members were invited by one London borough to come into schools to make books for their children. The books were translated and the whole activity enhanced the children's status. Moreover, the staff discovered relevant new information about the children's cultural worlds. Another important outcome of this project was that the parents became more involved with the school and this continued after the project ended. Trevor Cairney's accounts (1995, 2003) of his involvement with family literacy programmes that start from the child and recognise and build on home practices are helpful.

### Widening the focus of literacy learning in initial teacher education and continuing professional development

In the past ten years in the UK, training for new and serving teachers has involved familiarisation of centrally imposed initiatives and pedagogies. This has left little time for practitioners to engage in critical reflection on the more complex aspects of becoming literate or question assumptions and understandings about how and why deficit views of certain groups can exist.

Literacy in the Foundation Stage is currently embodied in the curiously named *Simple View of Reading* (DfES, 2006). This advocates moving through a pre-ordained skills based linear programme of 'synthetic phonics' as the universal approach to teaching reading. Consequently an educational philosophy that makes alternative funds of knowledge count is even more crucial if children's individual routes to literacy are to be developed. However, the report also recommends that children must be learning within 'a broad and rich language curriculum' (p70), and settings would do well to define what they understand by this term if they have not already done so. This is surely where space can be developed to see the process from the child's point of view and develop opportunities for children to make connections with home and recognise their unique literate identities.

Whole staff development on diversity, equality and English as an additional language can directly influence philosophy and practice. CPD on these issues can help the nursery team to focus on the importance of respecting and drawing on all children's diverse home experiences so they can develop relationships with children that will support their learning and help them feel positive about themselves.

## Practical strategies for developing young children's literacy
### Policies and guidelines

- Check existing policies on language and literacy, partnership with parents and equalities. How fully is the diversity of children's home literacy experiences actively included and their strengths positively recognised? Are policies available for parents and are they translated into the main languages in the setting?

- Look at the guidelines for discussions with parents and families. Are there suggestions for open questions that invite parents to talk about their expectations for children at nursery and their experiences at home?

- Evaluate displays and check that they do not reinforce stereotypes. Consider how they reflect the diversity of home experiences and communicate the message that knowing about children at home is seen as an important part of the jigsaw by staff who are not looking for uniformity or 'correct' practices.

■ Think about how assessment procedures incorporate children's home experiences and languages. Individual profile books can include photographs of children engaged in literacy activities and direct and tangible examples of their drawing and mark making. These can act as a record of children's experiences, interests and achievements and a guide for monitoring their development and planning for their learning. Including examples from home as well as nursery will demonstrate and encourage the two way process between home and school and help children, parents and staff to make relevant links. Where possible these books should include the languages known in families.

### Finding about children's literacy experiences at home

■ Talk to parents and children about their home literacy experiences and whether some take place in different languages and scripts. Are there examples of these experiences and languages on display in the form of signs, texts or media resources and are they used to support discussions of this kind?

■ Hold a parents' meeting or mount a display to acknowledge the different literacy experiences children have at home and attribute status and value to them. If possible, use photographs to show the range of experiences and emphasise how important they are for developing children's understanding of literacy. Involve parents in setting up these meetings and develop contact with community representatives who might be instrumental in supporting families who do not feel confident to contribute to the life of the nursery.

■ When planning, making observations and assessments, take account of information from parents about home literacy practices in all the relevant languages. Look for the connections children are already making with their interests and pre-occupations at home or where they encounter tensions. Note and plan responsively to support and develop the use of scripts and texts and employ children's strategies and patterns of interaction that will help them make links between the worlds of home and school. Talk to parents regularly about what their children have been doing in school so that those connections are made more explicit.

### Promoting multilingualism

■ Plan for a whole staff focus on multilingualism to create opportunities to discuss ideas and resources and explore appropriate strategies for individual children. Local Ethnic Minority Achievement (EMA) teams could be asked to advise on how to ensure staff commitment to supporting the development of children's first languages as a major means of expression and intellectual growth and also their learning of English. Discuss how this commitment can be made evident to parents and families.

■ Ensure that bilingualism is actively encouraged and promoted. Find out which languages children understand, speak or are learning to be literate in. Make sure these are represented in displays and in dual language texts. Make this language diversity a focus for discussion with all children and integral to nursery life by including all the relevant languages and scripts in displays. Give the languages the children know status by inviting parents or bilingual members of staff to tell stories or read aloud in them. Have dual language audiotapes and CDs available with accompanying books. Enlist the support of staff, parents and older children to record them in their home languages.

■ Employ bilingual members of staff who share some of the children's languages and can understand bilingual/bicultural experience at first hand. Their presence can create an important link to school for the children and they are often able to act as cultural mediators for parents (Drury, 2007). Ensure that they are fully involved in the cycle of observation and planning and have a clearly equal role in the nursery team. Unequal power relationships between bilingual teaching assistants and monolingual teachers give messages to children and parents about the status of minority languages and cultures.

■ Ask families for examples of songs, rhymes and jingles they share with their children and which children who are not yet interested in focusing on picture books at story times enjoy. The songs allow children to hear a familiar language, enhance their access to English and are a way of making links with home. Songs can easily be learned by heart by all the children and echo the cultural strategy of recitation familiar to some. They can be recorded on tapes or CDs, or made into small books accompanied by photos or children's drawings for everyone to look at and sing to.

### Make the nursery philosophy open for parents

■ Check that the nursery's philosophy is explicit in meetings with parents and in booklets translated into their languages. For example staff will have a professional view on the role of play in learning in their setting or about how and why children are encouraged to be independent and autonomous learners. Give examples from day to day practice of how children are encouraged to learn at their own pace and from each other, but show that teaching does also take place through adult intervention. Mount a photographic display of all the opportunities for literacy learning that are promoted in the nursery.

### Multimedia and popular culture

■ Ask children to bring in videos, CDs or DVDs from home and play them in the nursery. Film the adult and children at storytime or record children's dramatic role play, especially if they are using props such as masks, so they can watch the films and talk about them. These recordings can also be used to show parents how their children play in the nursery and support discussions about what they are learning. Encourage the children to talk about characters from popular culture that interest them, developing links with literacy and making the characters a focus for planned activities. Jackie Marsh (2000) and Guy Merchant (2005) have both examined the positive effects of interventions based on children's interest in such characters.

■ Give the computer high priority and ensure that the children have a range of software as well as guided access to the internet to help them use what they know from home. Make sure all the children, both boys and girls, have experience of engaging with multimedia, and develop their existing knowledge of meaning making using sound, images, visuals and other information. Digital media offer opportunities to link up with children's knowledge and experience at home while capitalising on their interest and the potential for engagement.

■ Provide models of TV and film characters and favourite super heroes, to encourage small world play. Children can then be encouraged to discuss and create stories about the models which could be scribed and read at storytime. Make a small world book with the children using photos, drawings and labels of their super heroes, toys and film characters.

### Literacy materials from home

■ Invite children and families to bring materials from home. These could form part of an ongoing interactive display of the different ways children experience literacy in their families and communities.

Make the 'unofficial' texts of home official, such as mark making, drawing, materials from playing schools, more formal work in different languages, magazines, comics, books bought from local shops. Draw attention to new additions, different scripts etc on display. Making these artefacts the focus of discussion at group time will give them status as well as enhancing the status of the children who brought them in.

■ Encourage bookmaking in which children make books about themselves using photos and drawings. These might also include materials from home such as those mentioned above.

■ What arrangements could be made to incorporate resources from home into play based literacy activities so that children see familiar materials in the mark making area or next to the computer? Think about scenarios for the role play area that will allow children's home literacy experiences to be incorporated and for children to see themselves represented. For example, hairdressing salons which have magazines that include hair styles favoured by different ethnic groups, cafes with foods on the menu from a range of cultures, shops that sell boxes and packets brought from home with labels in different languages.

■ Puppets which represent a range of ethnicities can help children to feel more secure and give them a voice they may not feel confident to use for themselves. Observations of children incorporating dolls and puppets in their play may give information about some of the learning strategies and experiences that are familiar at home.

As always, the communication skills of nursery staff, their philosophy of learning and willingness to see themselves as working in partnership with parents and families are crucial. In an environment where the consistent message is that home practices count because they are part of the children's experience, all interactions, whether one to one or in a small group, are more likely to be productive. Staff can take the lead from children in making connections between their rich and varied literacy worlds.

# References

Barton, D. (2007) *Literacy. An introduction to the ecology of written language.* Oxford: Blackwell

Bernstein, B. (1990) *Class, Codes and Control, Volume 4: The structuring of pedagogic Discourse.* London: Routledge

Bernstein, B. (1996) *Pedagogy, Symbolic Control and Identity.* London: Taylor and Francis

Bourdieu, P. (1997) The forms of capital. In Halsey, A, Lauder, H, Brown, P. and Wells, A. (eds) *Education, Culture, Economy and Society.* Oxford: Oxford University Press

Browne, N. (1999) *Young Children's Literacy Development and the Role of Televisual Texts.* London: Falmer

Brooker, L.(2002) *Starting School: Young children learning cultures.* Buckingham: Open University Press

Cairney, T. (2003) Literacy within family life. In Hall, N, Larson, J. and Marsh, J. (eds) *Handbook of Early Childhood Literacy.* London: Sage

Cairney, T. (1995) *Pathways to Literacy.* London: Cassell

Cairney, T.H. and Ruge, J. (1998). *Community Literacy Practices and Schooling: Towards effective support for students (Vols 1 and 2)* Canberra: DEETYA

Compton Lilly, C. ( 2003) *Reading Families. The literate lives of urban children.* New York, NY: Teachers College Press

Cummins, J. (2000). *Language, Power, and Pedagogy. Bilingual children in the crossfire.* Clevedon, England: Multilingual Matters

DfEE/QCA (1999) *The National Curriculum for England. English Key Stages 1-4.* London: DfEE

DfES (2006) *Independent Review of the Teaching of Early Reading: Final Report,* Nottingham: DfES

DfES (2007) *The Early Years Foundation Stage Curriculum.* London: DfES

Drury, R. (2007) *Young Bilingual Learners at Home and at School: Researching multilingual voices.* Stoke on Trent: Trentham

Dyson, A.H. (2003) *The Brothers and Sisters Learn To Write. Popular literacies in childhood and school cultures.* New York, NY: Teachers College Press

Edelsky, C. (1996) *With Literacy and Justice For All. Rethinking the social in language and educa-tion.* New York: Taylor and Francis

Gee, J. (1996) *Social Linguistics and Literacies: Ideology in discourses.* 2nd edition. London: Falmer

Gee, J. (2000) New people in new worlds: networks, the new capitalism and schools, in Cope, B. and Kalantzis, M.(eds) *Multiliteracies. Literacy learning and the design of social futures.* New York: Routledge

Gregory, E. (2001) Sisters and brothers as language and literacy teachers: synergy between siblings playing and working together. *Journal of Early Childhood Literacy* 1 (3) p301- 322

Gregory, E. (2007) What counts as reading inside and outside school and with whom, how and where? in Bearne, E. and Marsh, J. (eds) *Literacy and Social Inclusion. Closing the gap*. Stoke on Trent: Trentham

Gregory, E. and Williams, A. (2000) *City Literacies*. London: Routledge

Gutiérrez, K, Baquedano-López, P. and Tejada, C. (2000) Rethinking diversity and hybrid language practices in the third space. *Mind, Culture and Activity* 6 (4) p286-303

Hall, N. and Robinson, A. (2003) *Exploring Writing and Play in the Early Years*. London: David Fulton

Heath, S.B. (1983) *Ways With Words: Language, life and work in communities and classrooms*. Cambridge, MA: Cambridge University Press

Hollindale, P. (1992) Ideology and the Children's Book in Hunt, P. (ed) *Literature for Children: Contemporary criticism*. London: Routledge

Kelly, C. (2008) Literacy As Social and Cultural Practice in an Urban Community: Self, Solidarity and Status. Unpublished PhD thesis, Goldsmiths, University of London.

Kenner, C (2000) *Home Pages: Literacy links for young bilingual children*. Stoke on Trent: Trentham

Kenner, C. (2004) *Becoming Biliterate. Young children learning different writing systems*. Stoke on Trent: Trentham

Krashen, S.D. (1985) *The Input Hypothesis: Issues and implications*. London: Longman.

Kress, G. (1997) *Before Writing: Rethinking the Paths to Literacy*. London: Routledge.

Leichter, H.J. (1984) Families as environments for literacy, in Goelman, H. Oberg, A. and Smith, F. (eds) *Awakening to Literacy*. Portsmouth NH: Heinemann.

Long, S. (2002) Tuning in to teacher-talk: a second language learner struggles to comprehend. *Reading, Literacy and Language* Vol 36 (3) p113 – 118.

Luke, A.and Kale, J. (1997) Learning through difference: Cultural practices in early childhood language socialization. In Gregory, E. (ed) *One Child Many Worlds, early learning in multicultural communities*. London: David Fulton.

Marsh, J. (2000) Teletubby Tales: Popular culture in the early years language and literacy curriculum. *Contemporary Issues in Early Childhood* Vol 1 (2) p119-136

Marsh, J. (2003) One way traffic? Connections between literacy practices at home and in the nursery. *British Educational Research Journal* Vol 29 (3) p.369-82

Marsh, J.(2005) (ed) *Popular Culture, New Media and Digital Literacy in Early Childhood*, London: RoutledgeFalmer.

Marsh, J. and Millard, E. (2000) *Literacy and Popular Culture. Using children's culture in the classroom*. London: Paul Chapman

Merchant, G. (2005) Barbie meets Bob the Builder at the workstation. In Marsh, J. (ed) *Popular Culture, New Media and Digital Literacy in Early Childhood*. London: RoutledgeFalmer

Minns, H. (1997) *Read It To Me Now*. Second edition. Buckingham: Open Up

Moje, E.B. McIntosh Ciechanowski, K. Kramer, K. Ellis, L. Carrillo, R. and Collazo, T. (2004) Working toward third space in content area literacy: An examination of everyday funds of knowledge and discourse. *Reading Research Quarterly* Vol 39 (1) p38 -70

Moll, L. Amanti, C. Neff, D. and Gonzalez, N. (1992) Funds of knowledge for teaching: Using a qualitative approach to connect homes and classrooms. *Theory Into Practice*, Vol 31 (1): 132 – 141

Pahl, K. (1999) *Transformations: Meaning making in nursery education*. Stoke on Trent: Trentham.

Robinson, M. (1997) *Children Reading Print and Television Narrative*. London: Taylor and Francis

Rogers, R. (2003 ) *A Critical Discourse Analysis of Family Literacy Practices. Power in and out of print*. Mahwah, NJ: Lawrence Erlbaum Associates.

Rogoff, B. (1990) *Apprenticeship in Thinking. Cognitive development in social contexts*, Oxford: Oxford University Press

Rogoff, B. (2003) *The Cultural Nature of Human Development*. New York: Oxford University Press

Scribner, S. and Cole, M (1981) *The Psychology of Literacy*. Cambridge MA: Harvard University Press

Siraj-Blatchford, I. and Clarke, P. (2000) *Supporting Identity, Diversity and Language in the Early Years*. Buckingham: Open University Press

Skutnabb-Kangas, T. (2000) *Linguistic Genocide in Education – or Worldwide Diversity and Human Rights?* NJ: Lawrence Erlbaum Associates.

Solsken, J. (1995) *Literacy, Gender and Work in Families and in School*. Norwood NJ: Ablex

Street, B.V. (1984) *Literacy in Theory and Practice*, Cambridge: Cambridge University Press

Street, B.V. (1995) *Social Literacies: Critical approaches to literacy in development ethnography and education*. London: Longman

Tabors, P. (1997) *One Child, Two Languages: A guide for pre-school educators of children learning English as a Second Language*. Baltimore: Paul Brookes Publishing

Taylor, D. and Dorsey-Gaines, C.(1988) *Growing Up Literate: Learning from inner city families*. Portsmouth NH: Heinemann

Volk, D. and de Acosta, M. (2004) Mediating networks for literacy learning. In Gregory, E, Long, S. and Volk, D. (eds) *Many Pathways to Literacy*. London: RoutledgeFalmer

Vygotsky, L. (1978) *Mind in Society*. Cambridge MA: Harvard University Press

Weinberger, J. (1996) *Literacy Goes to School*. London: Paul Chapman

Wood, D., Bruner, J. and Ross, G. (1976) The role of tutoring in problem-solving. *Journal of Child Psychology and Psychiatry,* Vol 17 p.89-100.

## Children's books

Alborough, J. (2006) *Where's My Teddy?* Walker Books

Carpenter, S. (1999) *The Three Billy Goats Gruff*. HarperCollins

Campbell, R (2003) *Where's Spot?* Picture Puffin

Campbell, R.(2007) *Dear Zoo*. Campbell Books

Carle, E. (2002) *The Very Hungry Caterpillar*. Picture Puffin

Cooke, T (1997) *So Much*. Walker Books

Coxon, M. (1996) *Where's My Kitten*? Picture Puffin

Ganeri, A. (2007) *From Seed to Sunflower*. Heinemann

Hutchins, P. (1988) *The Doorbell Rang*. Picture Puffin

Martin, B & Carle, E. (2007) *Brown Bear, Brown Bear, What Do You See?* Puffin

Murphy, J. (2007 ) *Peace At Last*. Macmillan

Murphy, J. (2007) *Whatever Next*. Macmillan

Noyes, E. (1994) *Ruff's Bone*. Living Books

Smith, T. (1990) *Amazing Lizards*. Dorling Kindersley

Trivizas, E. and Oxenbury, H. (2003) *The Three Little Wolves and the Big Bad Pig*. Egmont Books

Vipont, E. and Briggs, R. (2000) *The Elephant and the Bad Baby*. Picture Puffin

Yales, I. and Lewis, J. (1999) *The Enormous Turnip*. Ladybird

West, C. (2009 ) *Not Me Said The Monkey*. Walker Books

# Index

See May 3/11